Omnisubjectivity

Omnisubjectivity

An Essay on God and Subjectivity

LINDA TRINKAUS ZAGZEBSKI

OXFORD
UNIVERSITY PRESS

OXFORD
UNIVERSITY PRESS

Oxford University Press is a department of the University of Oxford. It furthers
the University's objective of excellence in research, scholarship, and education
by publishing worldwide. Oxford is a registered trade mark of Oxford University
Press in the UK and certain other countries.

Published in the United States of America by Oxford University Press
198 Madison Avenue, New York, NY 10016, United States of America.

CIP data is on file at the Library of Congress

ISBN 978-0-19-768209-8

DOI: 10.1093/oso/9780197682098.001.0001

Printed by Integrated Books International, United States of America

Dedicated to my niece and nephew,
Shivaun Cooney and Brendan Cooney

Hail, holy Light, offspring of heaven first-born,
Or of the eternal co-eternal beam
May I express thee unblamed? since God is light,
And never but in unapproached light
Dwelt from eternity

—Milton, Paradise Lost, bk. 3, 1.1.

Contents

Preface

This book develops ideas I have published in three papers on omnisubjectivity (Zagzebski 2008, 2013, 2016a). I have written it in a more personal style than what we usually find in books of philosophy. There are many arguments, but the book is also a personal testament, particularly in the last chapter. I intend the arguments to appeal to a wide range of theistic philosophers and readers with differing views on the nature of God because I believe that omnisubjectivity is compatible with many theological standpoints, and it is entailed by some of them. I write as a Christian, but I also refer to Judaism and Islam since I believe that their views on the nature of God should lead them to endorse omnisubjectivity. I hope that this work will generate discussion about omnisubjectivity within and between groups of religious philosophers who may differ in the particulars of theology, but who are alike in accepting belief in a supreme being.

I am grateful for many invitations to discuss omnisubjectivity while I was writing this book. They include a podcast interview for *The London Lyceum* with Jordan Steffaniak and Brandon Ayscue, November 2021; the Aquinas Lecture to the Dominican School of Philosophy and Theology, Berkeley, March 2022; a lecture on omnisubjectivity and trust in God delivered at Chapman University, May 2022; a paper on omnisubjectivity given to the British Society for Philosophy of Religion, October 2022; the Edith Stein Lecture given at Franciscan University of Steubenville, Ohio, October 2022; and a paper presented to the Philosophy of Religion study group at Rutgers, November 2022. I owe special thanks to the people who generously commented on parts of the book while

I was writing it, particularly Timothy Miller, Tim Mawson, Tasia Scrutton, Ryan Mullins, and John Crosby. I am grateful for my good fortune in knowing people like them, and I look forward to future conversations about omnisubjectivity. I know that this book will not be my last word, and it certainly will not be the last word of the people kind enough to read it.

Santa Fe, New Mexico
November 22, 2022

1

Subjectivity

1.1. The Reality of Subjectivity

What is everything? Is subjectivity something? I will argue in this book that subjectivity is something, that it is not reducible to anything in the world of objective facts, and therefore, if God grasps everything, it is not enough that God grasps all the objective facts. God must also grasp all the subjectivity there is.[1] I call that property omnisubjectivity. The metaphysical question of what exists, and the theological question of what God knows are the same question.

What I mean by subjectivity is consciousness as it is experienced by the subject of conscious states, not consciousness as an object of personal reflection or empirical investigation or theoretical description. The degree and kind of consciousness differs from one species to another, but in human beings the range of conscious states is enormous. All our waking moments and many of our sleeping moments are filled with subjective states. We see, we smell, we taste, we touch, we hear, we feel, we desire, we remember, we imagine, we think, we think some more, we decide, we anticipate the next moment and the one after, and the one far in the future; we become aware of an ongoing mood, perhaps vaguely, perhaps with attention.

When we are conscious, we are always, or almost always, conscious *of* something—the sun rising in the sky, the words we hear

---

[1] Here and throughout this book I use the term "grasps" as the most general term for the mind's successful contact with actual or possible reality, whether objective or subjective.

Omnisubjectivity. Linda Trinkaus Zagzebski, Oxford University Press. © Oxford University Press 2023.
DOI: 10.1093/oso/9780197682098.003.0001

spoken, the event we are remembering. Typically, the object is something outside of us. But the conscious experience is distinct from the object of the experience, and when we are reflective, we can become conscious of the conscious experience as an object of another conscious state. When we look at the sunrise, we can "turn around," so to speak, and look at ourselves looking at it. We might only observe our state with curiosity, but we might try to change it, and often we try to communicate it. There are good reasons to treat parts of our consciousness as objects; we do that in order to govern ourselves. But in so doing, we change our conscious state into a thing of a different kind. It did not come into existence as an object; it was part of ourselves as subjects. We can talk about a conscious state as it is experienced by a subject, and we can talk about it as an object. There is a sense in which the subjective state and the object are the same thing, but in another sense they are not. I am interested in the sense in which they are not.[2]

When we turn our conscious experience into an object, we might notice features of it that can be expressed in language, the same language we use in describing the experiences of other people. As Wittgenstein memorably argued, we cannot have a purely private language to talk about or even to think about our experiences (2009, sec. 243–271). Even if, *per impossibile*, we could develop a private language, we would not want to because we like to communicate our private states to other people in a language they can understand. We use a public language of objects in describing our experiences, whether we are describing them to ourselves or to others. That might make it tempting to think that if someone understands a complete description of one of our conscious states in the public language, they understand *what* the experience is. But there is an important difference between understanding an experience

---

[2] In Zagzebski (2021), ch. 5, I propose a way that memory allows us to turn our subjective states into objects of reflection, and to embed those objects into a larger conception of the objective world.

through its public "objective" description, and understanding the experience through having it. Anybody can understand the experience objectively described, but what they understand is not the same as what you grasp when you have the experience. Your subjectivity is your consciousness as that consciousness is experienced from your first-person perspective, as the bearer of the experience. Other people are also subjects, and we sometimes want to understand them the way they understand themselves. It is a mystery how one subject can grasp another subject as a subject, not as an object. It is a mystery even when God is the grasping subject. That is the topic I will explore in this book.

What should we say about the difference between your first-person awareness of your conscious state and the awareness of your state as an object accessible by both yourself and others? One approach to addressing this issue is to examine the way we use personal pronouns. Linguists call the pronouns "I," "you," and "he/she/they" semantic primes because they have found that these words are universal—lexicalized in every language, they are innate rather than learned, and they are primitive in that they cannot be defined using other words.[3] We use the first-person pronoun when we express ourselves as a subject, and we use third-person pronouns and names when we treat something as an object. The difference in these uses is deep in human thought about the self and the world. It is one indication that there is a fundamental difference between experiencing oneself as a subject and experiencing oneself as an object in a world of objects. Similarly, there is a difference between experiencing someone else as a subject and experiencing them as an object in a world of objects.

In support of this difference, some philosophers have argued that a proposition expressed by using the indexical "I" is not equivalent to any proposition in the third person. To borrow a famous example that comes from John Perry (1979), if sugar is coming out

---

[3] See ground-breaking work on semantic primes by Anna Wierzbicka (1972, 1996).

of a hole in a sack in my supermarket cart and I come to know the proposition I express by

(1) "I made a mess in the market and everybody is staring at me,"

what I know is arguably different from what I and other people know that is expressed by

(2) "Linda Zagzebski made a mess in the market and all the bystanders are staring at her."

The sentences (1) and (2) are about the same event, but (1) is in the first person whereas (2) is in the third person. Are they just a different form of words to express the same proposition? One reason to think that they do not express the same proposition is that when I stop myself short and turn the sack over to stop it from spilling, my behavior can be explained by my knowledge of (1) but not by my knowledge of (2), unless the latter is supplemented by my knowledge that I am Linda Zagzebski, which reintroduces the indexical "I." The same point applies to my first-person reactive attitudes—being embarrassed, being annoyed with myself, feeling frustrated that I am losing time. Third-person reactions are quite different. Nobody else is embarrassed when they see that I spilled the sugar unless they are embarrassed *for* me, assuming my first-person viewpoint in their imagination. This is one reason to think that what we express in first-person sentences like (1) is not identical to what we express in third-person sentences like (2).[4]

So, should we say that (1) and (2) express two different propositions? Perry rejected that conclusion. He argued that when

---

[4] Perry (1979) argues that our motivations to behave in certain ways like the ones I have mentioned depend upon indexical rules of translation between subjective (first-personal) and objective (third-personal) understandings. The connection between belief and action and the first-person pronoun is discussed by Manuel Garcia-Carpintero (2017).

I know what I express by (1) and somebody else knows what they express by (2), we do know the same proposition, but the belief states by which we know that proposition differ. Other people can be in the belief state I am in when I know what I express by (1). That is when *they* are making a mess. What is unique to me is the combination of the two. Perry says: "Anyone can believe of John Perry that he is making a mess. And anyone can be in the belief state classified by the sentence 'I am making a mess.' But only I can have that belief by being in that state" (Perry 1979, 19).

In a later paper, Perry (2002) takes the position that the self is an epistemic category with no ontological import. The notion of *I* plays an epistemic role in the way we obtain information, but the information obtained does not give ontological significance to the first-person perspective. What he calls a "self-notion," the notion of being oneself, can be unlinked from a descriptive notion. Perry's self-notion was unlinked from his messy shopper notion before he realized that he was the one making the mess. Self-notions are not part of fundamental ontology.

Debates about the ontological status of the first-person perspective are usually motivated by the desire to prove or disprove scientific naturalism, or physicalism. Reductive naturalists like John Perry and David Lewis, and eliminative naturalists like Daniel Dennett and Thomas Metzinger, argue that the first-person perspective does not threaten a naturalistic ontology.[5] But that depends upon what an ontology is. If it is the fundamental objects given in a comprehensive account of the constitution of the universe, Perry and others might be right that the first-person viewpoint does not add anything to fundamental ontology. Subjectivity is not an object. Even so, first-person experience is something that exists. There is a difference between what is going on in the person's mind before

---

[5] Lynne Baker (2013, 49–56) argues that Perry has not successfully reduced first-person phenomena to third-person phenomena. In addition to her response to Perry, Baker responds to Dennett (1991), Metzinger (2003), and Lewis (1999).

and after she discovers that she made the mess herself, as Perry and most other naturalists agree. My point is that differences in what is going on in a person's mind are part of the universe, and ought to be knowable by a being who knows everything.

The world of facts does not encompass the whole world, even when the facts are expressed in the first person. Suppose that physicalism is a true theory about facts, and the fact that I feel frustrated at myself when I see that I made a mess is the same as the fact that certain events are going on in my nervous system. Somebody who knows the fact that those events are occurring also knows the fact that I am frustrated. But knowing that I am frustrated is not the same as knowing what it is like for me to feel frustrated. Facts *about* subjective states do not capture what it is like to be in that state, and what it is like to be in that state is something that exists.

At about the same time as Perry published his 1979 paper, David Lewis (1979) argued that propositions expressed by a sentence like (1), which he called *de se* propositions, differ from propositions expressed by sentences like (2), and he used their difference as a reason to conclude that *de se* propositions require us to give up either the common view that a proposition is accessible to more than one person, or the view that the truth of a proposition is absolute. He opted for the second alternative. If I made the mess referred to in (1), then (1) is true for me but not true for you. This generated a large literature on *de se* propositions because these propositions call into question the standard assumption that propositions are abstract entities with absolute truth values that are accessible to multiple minds.[6]

I have mentioned two interpretations of the difference between (1) and (2). On one interpretation, they express two different

---

[6] For skeptical responses to the arguments by Lewis (1979) and Perry (1979), see Cappelen and Dever (2013) and Magidor (2015). Garcia-Carpintero (2017) responds to these arguments in the paper mentioned above and argues that thoughts about oneself—*de se* thoughts—are not an illusion. They force us to revise traditional views about propositions.

propositions. On another interpretation, they express two different modes of apprehension of the same proposition. Notice that if either of these positions is true, someone who knows all the third-person facts does not know everything. If you know your subjective state from the inside, and they know your state from the outside, either *what* the two of you believe is different, or your states of believing are different. A being who knows everything must not only know what you believe, but that being must be able to tell the difference between your conscious state and the conscious state of a knower looking at you in the third person, which could be yourself.

There is a simpler way to approach the problem of subjectivity that does not involve positions on propositions and the grammar of personal pronouns. In a well-known story told by Frank Jackson (1986), we imagine that Mary has been confined to a black-and-white room her entire life. She has been educated through black-and-white books and videos, and she has come to know everything there is to know about the physical world by these means (Mary is the ultimate genius). There is no physical fact that Mary does not know, including all the physical facts about color and color perception, including her own color perception. But in that paper Jackson argues that Mary does not know everything there is to know because when she leaves her black-and-white room and sees in color for the first time, she learns something she did not know before. She comes to know *what it is like* to see color. Since physicalism, the theory that nothing exists but the physical, entails the thesis that if you know every physical fact you know everything there is to know, it follows that physicalism is false. This has come to be called "the knowledge argument."

I want to use this story to draw a different conclusion. Whether or not Mary comes to know a different fact when she leaves the room and sees in color for the first time, she is in a qualitatively different conscious state. The expression "what it is like" is just an informal way to make the point that something is different when she sees color than when she sees in black and white, and the difference is in her subjective state. The change in her subjective states is real, and a cognitively perfect being must be able to distinguish them, just as a cognitively perfect being must be able to distinguish my belief state when I utter (1) from anybody's belief state when they utter (2), whether or not (1) and (2) express different propositions. The story about Mary shows that there is a real difference between Mary's subjective states before and after she leaves the room. Jackson originally used the story of Mary to argue that reality cannot be reduced to the physical. My point is that it cannot be reduced to the objective. If physicalism is the thesis that the fundamental objects in the world are physical, that might be true for all I know. But if physicalism is the thesis that nothing exists but the physical, the Mary story shows that there is a feature of the universe that contrasts with the objective and cannot be grasped by grasping the objective facts. The problem is that the objective does not exhaust reality, whether or not the physical exhausts the objective.

In *Wings of Desire*, a 1987 movie directed by Wim Wenders, angels observe human life with sympathy but very little ability to intervene. They see the best and the worst of human existence, but as purely spiritual beings, they cannot experience what they observe. One angel, Damiel, watches a beautiful woman flying through the air on a trapeze and wonders what it feels like. He is curious to know why people laugh and what makes music enjoyable, and he wants to understand what goes on between human men and women, and why it is worth so much pain, whatever pain is. He falls in love with the trapeze artist and chooses to become human. He is delighted with his first human experience—being knocked on the head by an armored breastplate. He sees in color for the first time, and eagerly learns the names of the colors. He tastes coffee and enjoys rubbing his hands together in the cold. He then goes in search of the trapeze artist, who recognizes him in an instant as her true love. The story ends happily. He has no regrets at giving up his life as an angel.

What are we to make of this? Like Frank Jackson's story of Mary, we are meant to think that only a being who has had certain experiences can understand what they are, and we are also intended to think that any being who cannot have those experiences is deprived. Of course, Win Wenders is a human, and he cannot portray the point of view of angels, so it should not surprise us that human experience comes out looking better than angel experience in his movie. But whether or not it is better, it is clearly different.

Jackson (2003) changed his mind about the knowledge argument against physicalism, but his change of mind does not affect my point. Jackson argues that his mistake in his 1986 paper was in confusing intensional properties with instantiated properties. When we see something red, it is tempting to think that there is something out there in the world that is red and that our perceptual experience represents something that is the instantiation of red. But according to the intensional account of sensory states that he later accepted, there is no object that is red. We represent what we see as red, and we can be correct because that is how our sensory faculties operate when we see objects that have the physical properties of red objects. When Mary leaves her uncolored room and sees red for the first time, she represents objects as red for the first time, and there is a physicalist account of what happens in her brain when she represents objects as red, but she does not learn anything new about the world of red objects. Significantly, Jackson does not deny that she learns what a new experience is like. But Jackson says that this is no problem for physicalism since physicalists can allow that people are sometimes in states that represent things as having a property that is not part of physical ontology. What physicalists deny is that such properties are instantiated.

My argument about Mary does not depend upon positions on what properties are instantiated, what propositions are true, and whether Mary gains new knowledge of red objects when she leaves her uncolored room.[7] It is sufficient to maintain that Mary's

---

[7] My response also applies to Nagasawa's (2008) argument that the knowledge argument does not refute physicalism.

experience changes when she leaves her room, as she would undoubtedly exclaim excitedly upon leaving the room, and the angel
Damiel's experience changes when he becomes human. That difference is real, as even physicalists acknowledge, and that is the
difference that I am calling a difference in subjectivity. Mary is in
one subjective state while she is in the room and in a different and
distinguishable subjective state after she leaves the room. She can
tell the difference, and so should a being who knows everything. If
Mary can tell the difference, so should God.

I said that my conclusion about Mary and the mess in the store
does not turn on the issue of which propositions are true. That
brings up a number of issues about the nature of propositions. In
standard treatments of propositions, they are said to have the following features:

(1) A proposition is an abstract entity, distinct from the concrete
     world.[8]
(2) A proposition exists necessarily, with an absolute, un-
     changing truth value.
(3) A proposition is the content of a declarative sentence.
(4) A proposition can be grasped by multiple minds, and it is
     grasped through the intellect.
(5) All of reality is exhausted by the complete set of
     propositions. Actual reality is exhausted by the complete set
     of propositions true in the actual world. Possible reality is
     exhausted by the sum of maximally complete and consistent
     sets of propositions.

We have already seen some possible problems with this conception of possible worlds. David Lewis (1979) argued that *de se*

---

[8] This claim about propositions is common but not universal. David Lewis thought
of possible worlds as concrete objects. Each possible world is the maximal mereological
sum of individuals that are spatiotemporally related to each other and spatiotemporally
isolated from all others (Lewis 1986, 69–70).

propositions show that either (2) or (4) must be rejected. I believe that there is a problem in combining (3) and (5). If propositions are expressible in sentential form, and if subjectivity is a real phenomenon, subjectivity cannot be fully expressed by propositions. Mary can say, "Now I know what it is like to see color," but that is as close as she can get to expressing her experience. If someone else was with her in her black-and-white room, and she returned to the room and told them that she saw color for the first time, no matter what she says, she cannot convey the experience to them. Subjective experience goes beyond what is expressible propositionally, even when the proposition is expressed by using the first-person pronoun "I." Of course, we can say that there are propositions about subjective states that are not expressible in natural language, but that would mean that an enormous part of the world is inexpressible, and we lose much of the interest in talking about propositions.

Assuming that propositions are expressible in language, there are other reasons to think that propositions cannot fully express subjective reality. Consider the fact that we have no words for many of our subjective states. Sometimes we see nameless emotions represented in the faces of great paintings. The *Mona Lisa* is famous for having an enigmatic expression. We cannot identify the emotion, but we know it is there, and we might even recognize it as something we have felt ourselves. The same point applies to the feelings we have in listening to music. My vocabulary is probably larger than average, but I do not know how to verbally describe many, if not most, of the feelings that music elicits in me. Shortly before writing these words, I was listening to Mozart's clarinet concerto. People sometimes say that Mozart's music is emotionally elusive. They cannot tell whether it is happy or sad or something else. If we cannot tell, it is probably something else. I have no words for the feelings, at least not enough of them. It can be argued in a Wittgensteinian spirit that that means I do not know what I am feeling. Perhaps so, but the feelings are there whether I comprehend them or not. The existence of subjectivity is not primarily an issue about what we know, but about what exists. I believe these feelings exist because I am aware of them, at least vaguely, whether or not my awareness counts as knowledge.

According to (3), a proposition is something that can, in principle, be said. When combined with (5) we get the conclusion that everything that exists can be said. Do we know that what can be said about an experience leaves nothing out? Wittgenstein (1961) opens the *Tractatus* with the words, "The world is all that is the case. The world is the totality of facts, not of things." It is one thesis of this book that that is false.

Subjectivity is the experience of the world from inside a conscious mind. Objectivity is the world as it can be described from the outside. There is only one world, but it can be consciously grasped or described in these two different ways, but the way the world is grasped by some being is a part of the world. The grasping mind is in the world. Philosophical theories, scientific theories, theological theories discuss the world from outside conscious experience. They must do so because that is what theory requires. The point of a theory is to be a map of reality from an outside viewpoint that is communicable to somebody else. The outside viewpoint permits it to be the object of examination and discussion. But the outside viewpoint leaves the world of conscious experience behind. We sometimes hear that the outside view is as good as the inside view. That is doubtful, but even if it is true, the inside view is still something.

The objective/subjective distinction as I am using it is not the same as the distinction between the physical and the mental. Both distinctions arose after the Scientific Revolution and the change in philosophy that accompanied it. Mind and matter are two different kinds of phenomena, and ever since Descartes separated them and empirical science left consciousness out of nature, we have been left with the problem of how consciousness and unconscious nature connect. The subjective/objective distinction is different. Anything can be treated objectively. Consciousness is often treated objectively, and I have given examples of that. We treat our conscious states as objects in ourselves in order to govern ourselves and to communicate them to others. We think "My feeling was too extreme," or "I need to reconsider whether my belief is true." We also treat a conscious state as the object of empirical investigation in order to discover some of its features. Neurobiologists investigate the biological basis of consciousness. Psychologists investigate the relationship between subjective states of consciousness and behavior. So, the subjective world can be treated objectively. Conversely, the world of objective reality can be experienced by a conscious mind, and often is. Subjective states are frequently directed toward the world independent of the mind, and many philosophers believe that the only way we can access the objective world is through our subjective experience. Still, we know that the conscious mind is within the world. Our minds have the power to experience the world, including itself within the world, and the power to look at the world and the mind from outside a subjective experience of it. This way of contrasting subjectivity and objectivity interprets them as points of view that can be directed toward the same thing. But subjectivity and objectivity are not limited to points of view on the same thing. We can imagine a universe with objective nature and no conscious beings who have subjective states. Likewise, we can imagine a universe with beings who have subjective states but no objective nature, and who are incapable of treating their subjective states objectively in higher-order thoughts. We can imagine pure objectivity or pure subjectivity, but I assume that the created universe includes both the objective and the subjective, and that makes it very interesting.

Subjectivity became a focus of cultural awareness in the West long before anybody thought of a theory of propositions and the use of personal pronouns in language. It far predated the idea of "what it is like" to be a bat, or to feel pain, or to see red. The discussions in recent decades express some of our current attempts to bring subjectivity into philosophical discourse, but I think it would be helpful to look at the rise of the idea of subjectivity in Western history to help us see how the conception of reality changed when the division between subjectivity and objectivity became an important part of Western consciousness.

1.2. The Origin of the Subjective/ Objective Divide

The subjective/objective distinction arose late in our history, and it is interesting to notice how it arose.[9] Beginning in the Renaissance in art and literature, and about a century later in philosophy and science, people in numerous fields began to focus on the individual mind—to express it, and to investigate it. Before the modern era, consciousness was not perceived as a mystery; it was simply part of nature. In fact, if we go back as far as the mythopoeic era in ancient Egypt and Mesopotamia, it was the reverse.[10] Events in nature were interpreted as the product of conscious choice. The Nile decides to rise; the sun decides to set (Frankfort et al. 1946, 24). Human acts and acts of nature were thought to be on a par. Both were interpreted as personal, conscious, intentional, and permeated with emotion. When philosophy was invented, so was science, and there began a long and impressive era of the systematic treatment of all of reality as a single phenomenon governed by reason, the most important force in the universe.

It is tempting to say that in the long era from the beginning of philosophy up to the beginning of the modern age, everything in reality was treated as objective. Metaphysical accounts were always written in the third person. The pronoun "I" appears virtually

[9] This section is mostly a brief summary of Chapters 2 and 3 of my book, *The Two Greatest Ideas* (2021).

[10] Henri and Henriette Frankfort (1946) invented the term "mythopoeic" for a form of thought preceding the Greeks in which everything was interpreted as stories in which persons and emotions are fundamental. Similar ways of understanding the basic features of the world appear in the thought of many Native American tribes. For a good discussion, see Bruce Wilshire (2000).

nowhere in the pre-Socratics or Aristotle, and it appears in Aquinas only when he is quoting scripture passages. Plato wrote dialogues, of course, but they were written for their philosophical principles, not for any reflection on the importance of first-person experience, which does not seem to be an interest of Socrates or Plato. St. Augustine is often interpreted as a precursor to modern reflections on the self, but he does not put special philosophical or theological importance on the self, and his work did not lead to a division between two orders of reality: an objective order and a subjective order. So, it is not accurate to say that everyone thought of the world as objective since there was no idea of the subjective with which to contrast it. People thought of reality as one kind of thing and consciousness was a part of it. There was no "hard problem of consciousness" as some philosophers say today because it was taken for granted that the mind fits into nature.[11] The division between the world of consciousness and the world without consciousness began in the seventeenth century when philosophy and science changed in tandem.

The idea of subjectivity did not arise all at once. Descartes was not interested in anything distinctive about the self, and he was not interested in the difference between the first-person and the third-person viewpoints, but he revolutionized philosophy by creating a method in which all questions humans ask arise out of the individual ego's search for knowledge. Descartes intended to begin a revolution in philosophy, and he succeeded. He thought a revolution was needed to accompany the revolution in science. Modern science needed an epistemological foundation, and Descartes was eager to provide it. It is revealing that the full name of his *Discourse on Method* is *Discourse on the Method of Rightly Conducting One's Reason and of Seeking Truth in the Sciences*. In it, he lamented the

---

[11] The so-called hard problem of consciousness is the explanatory gap between the physical aspects of consciousness and the qualitative or phenomenal aspects of consciousness. The term was coined by David Chalmers (1995).

fact that even though philosophy had been cultivated for centuries by some of the most excellent minds, everything they wrote was in dispute, and "as to the other sciences, to the extent that they derived their principles from philosophy, I judged that one could not have built anything solid upon foundations having so little firmness." (*Discourse* 1 C:5). He then proceeded to describe what would make the foundations firm, and he introduced three treatises exemplifying his method: one on optics, one on geometry, and one on meteorology.

Empirical science produced a new method for studying nature, but it also produced a new interpretation of the nature that is studied. Nature as the object of modern science is the object of conscious observation, but ironically, it does not include consciousness and it is a closed causal system. It does not need interaction with anything outside of it such as God or a supernatural order for it to be complete. That eventually led some philosophers and scientists to think that physical science can produce a theory of everything, and that explains the attraction to physicalism. But physicalism made consciousness a puzzle, and it has led to a rift between those philosophers who are willing to reduce consciousness to the physical or eliminate it from ontology, and those who do not.

The revolution in subjectivity began before Descartes when it was discovered how subjectivity can be expressed in art and literature. When perspective geometry was brought to Florence in the fifteenth century, that made it possible for visual works to have a consciously chosen point of view. That in turn led to greater awareness of the existence of different points of view and the individual minds that possess them. Art not only became more realistic, it changed from the representation of a common vision that we see lavishly displayed in medieval cathedrals, to the expression of an original aesthetic. Art began to express an interior and singular point of view and it became much more common for works to be signed. Originality became a dominant value, whereas previously it would have been thought egotistical to call attention to oneself in one's creations.[12] The enormous variety in artworks created since the Renaissance are captivating partly because of the fascinating difference in the sensibilities they express. The self rose in importance when it became possible to express it.

There was also a revolution in literature. Thirty-six years before Descartes published the *Meditations*, Cervantes published the first part of *Don Quixote*, universally regarded as one of the most influential works of fiction ever written.[13] William Egginton (2016) argues that what made *Don Quixote* ground-breaking was the invention of "characters," each of whom is not just a type, but is like a real person with a subjective world of his own and a unique point of view (xix). We are so used to fictional characters who seem real that it can be surprising to notice how long it took for that idea to take hold of the human imagination.

In his important 1981 essay, "Epic and Novel," Mikhail Bakhtin contrasts the dominant literary form of ancient Greece and the Middle Ages with the dominant literary form of the modern era, and Bakhtin argues that the difference between the ancient epic and the modern novel reveals a transformation in human consciousness. He argues that in the epic the consciousness of the individual characters is not as relevant as the action (a point made by Aristotle in his interpretation of poetry),[14] and the consciousness of the listener or teller of the story is not relevant at all. In the

---

[12] In Emile Mâle's (1972) classic work on the medieval cathedral, he argues that the purpose of art in this period was to express a common vision. Art was never the exclusive creation of an individual talent; it was the product of what he calls "diffused genius" (4). In contrast, the art of a few hundred years later tells us very little about the thought of the day, but a great deal about the perspective of individuals.

[13] When the Norwegian Nobel Institute asked one hundred leading fiction writers from fifty-four countries to name the single most important literary work in history, more than half chose *Don Quixote*. No other work came close. (Reported by *Reuters* Wed, May 8, 2002. Reported the same day in the *New York Times* and the *Guardian*.)

[14] In *Poetics* ch. 9, Aristotle makes it clear that the characters are for the sake of the action, and the action is portrayed in a causal structure that is universal: "The objects the imitator represents are actions, with agents who are necessarily either good men or bad—the diversities of human character being nearly all derivative from this primary distinction" (1448a, 1–4).

novel, in contrast, the consciousness of the character is highly relevant and might even be the whole story, and the author is aware
of the reader's consciousness. We can identify with the characters
in novels and experience their lives with them. We enter into their
subjectivity and for a while we can adopt it as if it were our own.
Nothing like that happens with epic characters (1981, 32).

Bakhtin argues in another essay, "Forms of Time and Chronotype
in the Novel," that for the Greeks every aspect of human existence
could be seen and heard (Bakhtin 1981, 134). They did not distinguish what we call the internal from the external. For them, an
autobiography is the same as a biography; both are public (1981,
136). In Greek literature there are no deep soliloquies,[15] and no attention to individual uniqueness even in external descriptions. The
difference between inner subjectivity and the outer person did not
exist. Linguists tell us that the first-person pronoun is universal and
primitive, but the idea that there is anything about the *I* that is as interesting as the object of the *I's* awareness is not universal. Western
history evolved for millennia without it.

What I mean by the self is the bearer of subjectivity. It is not the
same as the *I*, which Descartes argued is a conscious substance. But
scrutiny of the *I* led to the idea of the self, probably beginning with
critiques of Descartes's argument that the *I* is a substance given by
Locke, Hume, and Kant, and particularly in the work of Fichte,[16]
who claimed that an account of subjectivity is necessary to solve
the problem that Kant lacked a unitary account of the self. As I read
Kant, he made a valiant effort to combine an objective treatment
of the human *person*, whose defining value is rationality, with the
value of the *self*, the self-conscious being whose defining value is

---

[15] Bakhtin claims that the public square is alive even in Augustine's *Confessions*,
which Bakhtin says must be "declaimed aloud" (135). He observes that it is nothing like
Hamlet's soliloquy, and it is far removed from Virginia Wolff's *Mrs. Daloway*.
[16] This claim is defended by Marcel Mauss in Carrithers et al. (1985, 22). That essay
gives an interesting discussion of the replacement of the person by the self. See Carrithers
et al. (1985, 21).

autonomy. Kant went to great pains to identify rationality with autonomy, but the historical consequence was a dramatic shift from the idea that the ground of morality is reason, understood as a force in the universe, to the idea that morality is grounded in the individual will, making the ultimate bearer of authority the self. The focus of attention in ethics and political theory, as well as in metaphysics, shifted to the self. Since it had already shifted in art and literature, the turn to the self, the possessor of subjectivity, was one of the great revolutions in human thought.

The idea of the uniqueness of the subjectivity of each self took much longer to develop. Charles Taylor (1991, 28–29) comments that Kant's student, Johann Herder, proposed that each of us has a unique way of being human, although Herder does not connect personal uniqueness with subjectivity. By the twentieth century, the prominent theologian, Hans Urs von Balthasar (1986), identified dignity with the irreplaceability of the person, not with their human nature as such (1986, 18), and a focus on the uniqueness of persons appears in the Personalist movement of the first half of the twentieth century, particularly in the writings of Karol Wojtyla before he became Pope (2008), in which he explicitly connected the uniqueness of persons with subjectivity.

The idea that persons are unique and that the locus of their uniqueness is in their subjectivity is widespread in Western culture, so its sources must have been many. We now appreciate individual differences in consciousness and attempt to understand them. That extends to people with disabilities who are not able to exercise to the fullest the common property of persons objectively described— their rationality. Only philosophers get excited about rationality, but everybody is fascinated with the subjectivity of other persons and the differences among them. The idea of subjectivity and its uniqueness has flowed deeply into our culture.

In giving my interpretation of the origin of the contrast between subjectivity and objectivity in Western thought, I am not urging readers to adopt my historical thesis in any detail, which clearly has been very brief. My purpose is to call attention to the fact that the contrasting notions of objectivity and subjectivity did not always exist. I think that it is important to see that the current problem of relating them arose because of historical contingencies. I hope that that will give us a sense of humility about what the two notions mean and their relative importance. I will return to that issue in the last chapter.

I believe that each person's subjectivity is unique and necessarily so, but the idea of subjectivity and its importance does not require that assumption. My main point is that subjectivity is a different kind of phenomenon than objectivity, and a being who grasps nothing more than the world of objective facts does not grasp all that exists, and he does not grasp something of deep value in the creation. When the dichotomy between subjectivity and objectivity was created, it produced one of the deepest of all philosophical problems—how subjectivity and objectivity connect. It also created the theological problem of how God grasps both the subjective and the objective aspects of his creation. The way the subjective and the objective connect in the mind of God reflects the way they connect in reality. To repeat, "What is everything?" and "What does God know?" are the same question.

1.3. The Scope of Subjectivity: Consciousness in God and Creatures

How far does subjectivity extend in the universe? Consciousness as we know it is connected with our biology, but it is easy to postulate the existence of nonbiological beings with consciousness. According to traditional conceptions of God, God is more conscious than any other being, but he has no body. Leaving aside Wim Wenders, few people talk about angels these days, but traditionally they also were described as nonphysical but conscious and more intelligent than humans. Presumably, having a certain kind of functioning biology is sufficient for consciousness even if it is not necessary. We perceive consciousness in many species of animals from acquaintance with them, and we can develop relationships with them that includes mutual communication of conscious states. Alternatively, we may infer the consciousness of animals from their neurological systems, and that has led to a number of disputes such as the debate about whether fish feel pain and whether there is consciousness in the octopus. It is intriguing that Sylvia Medeiros et al. (2012) discovered that cephalopods have both a quiet sleep state and a periodic active sleep state with rapid eye movements, suggesting that the octopus dreams.[17] Studies of many other animals, including some reptiles, apparently indicate different levels of consciousness not previously recognized.

Even if consciousness is ubiquitous, it does not follow that the possession of a self is just as ubiquitous, and if a self is the bearer of subjectivity, the range of subjectivity in the universe might be more limited than the range of consciousness. I assume that having a sense of self requires awareness of conscious continuity. Presumably some conscious creatures lack that sense, so they do not have subjectivity if we are using human subjectivity as the standard. Nonetheless, their consciousness is still something that should be knowable to God.

It is apparent that there are degrees of consciousness, and the sense of self might not be an all-or-nothing feature of the world. In humans, the consciousness of the fetus develops in stages, and there is research that indicates that the fetus has subjectivity and a minimal sense of self by the third trimester.[18] This is another

---

[17] *My Octopus Teacher* (2020) is a fascinating documentary about the year that filmmaker Craig Foster spent developing a relationship with a young wild octopus in a South African kelp forest. The ability of the octopus to engage in personal communication is unmistakable.

[18] See Rochat (2011) for a summary of studies on the subjectivity of newborns. Rochat writes: "Striking, and arguably among the major discoveries in developmental psychology over the past thirty years, is the fact that most of what is demonstrated in newborns is also shown in healthy fetuses during the last trimester of gestation: they habituate, learn, store experiential information, demonstrate comparable thresholds across sensory modalities. Furthermore, what they learn in the womb is readily transferable *ex*

example of a continuum. Having thoughts about one's conscious states requires a much higher order of consciousness than merely possessing conscious states. The ability to think of one's pain *as* pain is different from the ability to feel pain, and the human fetus, as well as other animals, can feel pain but cannot think of their pain as pain. Language is necessary for the thought, "This is pain," or "I am in pain," and the memory of previous conscious states is necessary for integrating these states into one's awareness of self. It is interesting that drugs like Versed induce amnesia so that the pain of a medical procedure is not remembered (when it works). I have heard people say that if you don't remember the pain, that's the same as if it didn't happen. I don't agree with that, but I agree that there is a difference between having a sensation and forming a thought about the sensation that is then incorporated into one's narrative of the self. A sensation that is neither conceptualized nor remembered is still something, a part of the world as a whole, and hence a potential object of knowledge. Similarly, the sensation of an animal that cannot form thoughts about its sensations is something that ought to be knowable by a being who knows everything. I imagine that fish and octopuses have no sense of self, but they might have subjectivity in a weak sense, and some of my arguments in the next chapter would apply to them if there is such a thing as what it is like for a fish to have a hook in its mouth, or what it is like for an octopus to dream, or what it is like for a third-trimester fetus to be aborted.[19]

Lynne Rudder Baker (2013) distinguishes the simple first-person perspective from what she calls the "robust first-person perspective," which is the capacity to think of oneself as oneself, as the object of one's thought (xix). Self-consciousness requires the robust first-person perspective, and it is this perspective that she takes to

utero" (62–63). They also have a proprioceptive sense of their own body as a distinct unified entity among other discrete entities in the environment (2011, 66). Both proprioceptive and vestibular sensitivities are well developed and operational at birth (2011, 68).

[19] See Carruthers (1998) for an interesting discussion of animal subjectivity.

demonstrate the failure of reductive and eliminative naturalism. The distinction between the simple first-person perspective and the robust first-person perspective is pertinent to the issue I am raising about the degree and kind of consciousness necessary for subjectivity. If subjectivity is the interior of a self, and if there are conscious beings who cannot think of the I *as* an I, then there are conscious beings that do not have subjectivity. But consciousness even without the robust first-person perspective is still something, something that distinguishes a fish from a rock. A being who knows everything must grasp the conscious state of the fish as well as the subjective state of the human person. According to the higher-order theory of phenomenal consciousness, there is no "what it is like" for animals that cannot form thoughts about the experience. So allegedly, there is no such thing as what it is like for an octopus to be in the state of active sleep or for a fish to feel a hook in its mouth. I am arguing that as long as there is *some* difference between the deep sleep state and the REM state of an octopus, and there is some difference between the fish's feeling before and after it gets hooked, that difference must be known by a being who knows everything.

What about artificial intelligences? The issue of whether a robot can be conscious has been hotly disputed, and nothing I say in this book depends upon the outcome of that controversy, but it is interesting that the possibility that consciousness can exist in non-biological beings created by humans also suggests the possibility that the potential for consciousness is inherent in matter and that it becomes actualized at a certain level of organization. Perhaps it exists in an incipient form in all matter, a form of panpsychism. We know very little about how far subjectivity extends in the universe, but we know at a minimum that it exists in abundance and that it is a significant feature of human lives, both individually and collectively. In fact, I think it is not much of an exaggeration to say that human living *is* subjectivity.

Humans, angels (if they exist), and at least some animals have subjectivity, and it is possible that beings with subjectivity can be created that are not normal biological organisms, such as intelligent robots. The extent of subjectivity deserves much more attention than I can give it, but the purpose of this book is to focus on the subjectivity of one being in particular—God. Does God have subjectivity? Surely, only a being with subjectivity can grasp the subjectivity of another being, so if God grasps our subjectivity, God must have subjectivity. I take that to mean that there is something it is like to be God. It also follows that God has an *I*, which is a personal perspective, and I will argue that that has implications for the way we should understand the Trinity. We think of subjectivity as the experiential aspect of being, so I conclude that God has experience. It may be misleading to say that God has experience if God is timeless and experience means going through a sequence in time, but I think that we can at least say that God is aware of being God and is aware of the world in its entirety from the divine viewpoint.

Scripture is full of God speaking in the first person, and ever since people got the idea of subjective consciousness, it is impossible to read the Bible without thinking of God as having subjectivity. God speaks to Abraham when he instructs him to leave for Canaan and after he arrives (Gen. 12), and God addresses Abraham to promise him the entire land of Canaan (Gen. 13). He speaks to Moses in the burning bush in Exodus 3:14, uttering the enigmatic, "I Am Who Am. This is what you are to say to the Israelites: 'I AM has sent me to you.' "[20] The insistence on the first-person pronoun when the report would normally require the use of the third person is very interesting because it makes the use of "I" unmistakable and attributes an "I" to the God speaking to Moses. God makes a personal Covenant with the Jews. He makes promises, offers comfort and guidance, lays down commandments, and acts in many other interpersonal ways that imply that he has subjectivity. In the New Testament, Jesus sometimes uses the first person in a way that has

---

[20] This translation is from the New American Bible. The New Revised Standard Version is close: "I Am Who I Am. This is what you are to say to the Israelites: 'I AM has sent me to you.' "

deep theological significance, as when he says "I am the way, the truth, and the life. No one can come to the Father except through me" (John 14:6). The God of scripture has subjectivity, and the subjectivity of God is by no means a trivial flourish to make God easier for humans to understand. Subjective viewpoints can be shared, and it did not take a modern philosophical revolution for people to realize that.

It must be admitted that the philosophical tradition is much thinner on the subjective side of God than we find in scripture. Aquinas is a good example. He says that God is pure being, which sounds abstract, but he explicitly states that God has life. God *is* his own act of living (SCG 98:2), and since understanding and willing are ways of living, God is his own act of willing and understanding (SCG 98:3), which certainly seem to be conscious states. Aquinas also attributes to God particular states that are intrinsically subjective. He says that God has joy and delight (SCG 90) and, of course, love (SCG, ch. 91). Later we will look at the issue of whether God has feelings, but it seems to me that if God is a living being who understands, loves, and has joy, God must have subjectivity.

An important reason for attributing subjectivity to God is the connection between subjectivity and personhood, but traditionally, the property of rationality was thought to be the property that distinguishes a person from a nonperson. Boethius's definition of a person in the sixth century became the *locus classicus* for later accounts of personhood: A person is an individual substance of a rational nature (Boethius 1973, 85). Aquinas used this definition in arguing that personhood belongs to God preeminently:

> *Person* signifies what is most perfect in all nature—that is, a subsistent individual of a rational nature. Hence, since everything that is perfect must be attributed to God forasmuch as His essence contains every perfection, this name *person* is fittingly applied to God; not, however, as it is applied to creatures, but in a more excellent way. (ST I q. 29, a. 3, corpus)

If we use Boethius's definition of a person, the God of Aristotle, the Unmoved Mover (UM), is a person. The UM is a purely rational being, whose thinking is of itself. "Its thinking is a thinking on thinking" (*Meta* XII, 9 1074b 34). However, Aristotle says that the UM is a living thing and that its life is the most pleasant and the best of all (*Meta* XII, 7 1072b 19–29). That sounds like a being with subjectivity. But Aristotle also says that in God there is no distinction between thought and the object of thought, which is a distinction only in material beings (1075a 3). God is absolute self-consciousness, completely unaffected by anything outside itself, and God has no relationships with other beings. Aristotle's God would be a person on Boethius's definition since it is clearly an individual substance of a rational nature, but not on definitions that build relationality with other conscious beings into the definition of a person, the dominant conception in the Christian tradition. This is an important point because if subjectivity is the inside of a person, the conditions for being a person affect the issue of divine subjectivity.

Perhaps it is possible in some sense of possible that there is a God who does not think of itself as *I* and has no relations to other conscious beings, but the God of Judaism, Christianity, and Islam is a person with a self (or three selves), and God enters into relationships with human beings and possibly other conscious beings. I have said that only a God with subjectivity can be omnisubjective. I think that we have seen other considerations from the monotheistic traditions that strongly imply that God has subjectivity. I have no idea what it is like to be God, but I think that there is such a thing as what it is like—on the inside—to be God.

1.4. The Importance of Subjectivity

What difference does it make if God has subjectivity? Would it change anything in our theology or our ethics or our religious life?

I think it changes a lot. A well-known objection to the kind of theology that heavily borrows from the history of Christian philosophy is the complaint that the so-called God of the philosophers differs from the God of scripture, and that the high metaphysical conception of God that we see in Augustine and Aquinas and continuing through a long line of analytic philosophers of religion into the twentieth and twenty-first centuries is not sufficiently grounded in scripture, and sometimes makes God appear to be something akin to Aristotle's Unmoved Mover, or even worse, Plato's Form of the Good. I think that there are answers to this worry, but one of the things I like the best about the attribute of omnisubjectivity is that it directly connects the high metaphysical view of God as the supremely perfect being with the Biblical narrative of a being who personally interacts with human beings, sharing in their lives with its trials and suffering. When God calls Moses in Exodus, Yahweh says: "I have observed the misery of my people who are in Egypt; I have heard their cry on account of their taskmasters. Indeed, I know their sufferings, and I have come down to deliver them from the Egyptians" (Ex 3:7). The word "know" in ancient Hebrew means intimate acquaintance, not only propositional knowledge, so the text strongly implies that God has awareness of what the Israelites' suffering was like.[21] This is a God who is intimately acquainted with suffering, a personal God whom human beings can love, not just adore.

I have argued that subjectivity is real and distinct from the world objectively described. I want to say also that it is important. It is not something we can dismiss. In some contexts, subjectivity is defined as what depends for its existence upon consciousness, or more specifically, the consciousness of the individual, while objectivity is what does not depend upon consciousness. Once the objective/

---

[21] Marcel Sarot (1991, note 3) quotes this passage and comments that it suggests that God knows what suffering feels like. He refers to Fretheim (1989) for the meaning of "know" in ancient Hebrew.

subjective distinction became seared into the philosophical mind by the time of the Enlightenment, the so-called objective view of anything outside ourselves was thought to be superior because it is free from the limitations of the individual perspective. In fact, the term "the God's-eye view of reality" has sometimes been used by atheists as well as by theists to refer to a view of everything from no point of view at all, or what Thomas Nagel (1986) has called "the view from nowhere." The idea that the view from nowhere is superior to the view of an individual person has been under attack for some time, but it cannot be rejected out of hand. There *is* something important about seeing from a point of view beyond our own. Most of us need to stretch our minds to appreciate the world as experienced by others, and there are reasons why we need to stretch our minds even farther to understand the world as it is unaffected by consciousness of any kind. We want airplanes to fly; we want to understand disease; we want to be able to predict the weather. Grasping minds does not help with that. But grasping minds helps with much that we care about that is just as real as the workings of unconscious nature.

The way we distinguish the subjective from the objective need not make the objective world primary. If God is conscious and is the creator of the world, the world is the product of God's consciousness. That means that the subjectivity of God is more basic than anything else in existence except God's own existence. What we think about the subjectivity of God affects what we think about reasons for the creation of the world and God's relation to it, as well as the doctrines of the Trinity and the Incarnation. I will discuss that in Chapter 6.

I have defined omnisubjectivity in a way that makes the sharing of subjectivity go only one way—God's grasp of our mental states, but I believe that it is possible for God to share his subjectivity with us. Traditionally, sanctifying grace has been defined as sharing in the divine life, a doctrine that is mysterious given that we are not capable of divine understanding. Aquinas argues that in heaven our eyes are opened to a vision of the divine essence in the Beatific Vision. St. Paul says that "now we see in a mirror, dimly, but then we will see face to face. Now I know only in part; then I will know fully, even as I have been fully known" (1 Cor. 13). The promise of knowing everything fully through seeing God who fully sees us is the zenith of intersubjectivity. Aquinas says that God's essence is being. I will propose that God's being is subjectivity, and it is in seeing God's subjectivity that we have the vision Aquinas imagines as our heavenly reward.

2
Why God Must Be Omnisubjective

2.1. Introduction

There are many reasons why the God of traditional Christianity must be omnisubjective. Most of the reasons I will discuss also apply to the way God is understood in Judaism and Islam, and I will include some references to sacred texts in all three religions, but my arguments are mostly theoretical. I will begin by arguing that the attributes of omniscience and omnipresence entail omnisubjectivity. These arguments would apply to any religion in which there is an omniscient or omnipresent being, including monotheistic Hinduism.[1] I will also argue that omnisubjectivity is presupposed by common practices of prayer, and it is strongly implied by both divine love and divine justice. I will defer my argument that omnisubjectivity is possible to Chapter 3. If omnisubjectivity is entailed by the attributes of omniscience and omnipresence but is an impossible property, then omniscience and omnipresence are impossible. Likewise, if omnisubjectivity is impossible but is a presumption of common practices of prayer, then those practices are incoherent. If our understanding of God's love and justice imply omnisubjectivity, the impossibility of omnisubjectivity would force us to modify the way we understand divine love, justice, and providential care.

In Chapter 1 I looked briefly at the history of the rise of the idea of subjectivity and its contrast with the idea of the objective world.

---

[1] See Gavin Flood (2020) for a history of the rise of Hindu monotheism, and the later development of the idea of a transcendent God that is omniscient and omnipresent.

Omnisubjectivity. Linda Trinkaus Zagzebski, Oxford University Press. © Oxford University Press 2023.
DOI: 10.1093/oso/9780197682098.003.0002

In the era in which sacred texts were written, the idea of subjectivity did not exist, nor did it exist in most of the era in which the philosophy and theology to which I will be referring was written.[2] But that does not mean that there was no discussion of human minds. There was plenty of discussion of minds, but those discussions were not conducted against a background of a dichotomy between the subjective and the objective. That distinction and the need to explain how objectivity and subjectivity connect is a modern problem. One of the ironies of the history of philosophy is that the modern turn to the consciousness of the self accompanied the Scientific Revolution, and both Descartes and the British empiricists eagerly embraced the task of producing a philosophical foundation for empirical science in the individual conscious mind,[3] but when it turned out that empirical science could claim to produce a complete conception of the world only if consciousness can be either eliminated from that conception or reduced to the physical, consciousness became an embarrassment.

For the purposes of this book, many of the disputes that have arisen about consciousness can be bypassed. I mentioned in discussing Frank Jackson's story of Mary that the existence of Mary's subjectivity does not commit us to positions on which properties are instantiated, what propositions are true, and whether Mary gains new knowledge of the world outside her mind when she leaves her uncolored room. Subjectivity is probably

---

[2] I will be making frequent reference to Aquinas, whom I believe did not have the idea of subjectivity, but I will argue that Aquinas's arguments directly lead to omnisubjectivity. For an interpretation of Aquinas according to which he did have the idea of subjectivity and possibly even omnisubjectivity, see Anthony Flood (2014) and (2018), ch. 6. Flood argues that human persons have subjectivity because of our participation in God.

[3] The German Idealists also aimed to connect philosophy with the new science. Schelling even attempted a scientific proof for idealism, and Hegel's project of putting together the philosophy of nature and the philosophy of spirit in what he called the *Realphilosophie* was meant to fold natural philosophy, cultural philosophy, and empirical science together into a common science. See Gadamer (1981, 7) for a discussion of this point.

not a property, and awareness of one's subjectivity might not be directed at propositions. In fact, it almost certainly is not. Whether that awareness constitutes knowledge also depends upon whether knowledge is a state directed only at propositions. At the end of this book, I will offer some speculations on the place of subjectivity in a comprehensive conception of the world as a whole, but in this chapter, I want to look at why God must be aware of our subjectivity in all its aspects, including the way the subjectivity of one creature differs from that of another.

2.2. Omniscience

Omniscience is the property of knowing everything, but what does it mean to know everything?

One issue debated by medieval Christian and Muslim theologians was whether God knows particulars. Arguably, God would know everything if God knew only the universals that are instantiated in the created world. Aquinas took that view seriously because he accepted Aristotle's position that things are singular only because of their matter, but the objects of knowledge are nonmaterial (ST I q. 14, a. 11 obj. 2). For instance, one human being differs from another only because of the matter of which their bodies are composed. Since matter is not an object of knowledge, it seems to follow that God would know everything knowable about you and me as long as he grasps our shareable human nature. But surely that is a pale kind of knowledge.

Aquinas's response is that it is part of our perfection to know singular things, and he remarks that even Aristotle says that it would be incongruous if anything known by us should be unknown by God (ST I q. 14 a. 11 corpus). However, God does not know by abstraction, as we do, but by being the principle by which all things exist, whether material or immaterial (ST I q. 14 a. 11 reply obj 1). God's knowledge extends as far as His causality extends (ST I q. 14

a. 11 corpus). Furthermore, God knows each thing in its distinct-
ness from other things.

> To have a proper knowledge of things is to know them not only in
> general, but as they are distinct from each other. Now God knows
> things in that manner. Hence it is written that He *reaches even*
> *to the division of the soul and the spirit, of the joints also and the*
> *marrow, and is a discerner of thoughts and intents of the heart; nei-*
> *ther is there any creature invisible in His sight.* (Heb 4:12.13, italics
> in original; *ST* I q. 14 a. 6 corpus)

In the *Summa contra Gentiles* Aquinas writes: "God knows whatever is found in reality. But this is to have a proper and complete
knowledge of a thing, namely, to know all that there is in that
thing, both what is common and what is proper" (*SCG* I 50:2).
A few articles later he says, "Again, whatever God knows, he
knows most perfectly" (*SCG* I 50:5). So, Aquinas is arguing that
God knows everything in its particularity as well as what it shares
with other things, and he knows each particular thing perfectly.
Nonetheless, God's knowledge is not broken up into discrete bits
the way it is for us. God knows all particulars directly and in one
grasp (*ST* I q. 14 a. 7).

Contemporary believers no doubt agree with Aquinas that
knowing universals is not sufficient for knowing everything, and
they probably also believe that the difference between the general
and the particular extends to the human mind. It follows that God
must know the particularity of a human mind in addition to each
mind's shareable features. Aquinas does not seem to be interested
in the uniqueness of minds, but he quotes from Proverbs: "All the
ways of a man are open to His eyes" (Prov. 16:2). Given that he has
argued that God knows particulars, I take that to imply that God
not only knows what it is like to see the color red in general, but he
knows what it is like for you right now to see a certain red tomato,
and how that differs from what it is like for your companion to see

that red tomato, if there is any difference. He knows how your anxiety feels to you, not just how anxiety feels in general. He knows each individual feeling of joy, fear, frustration, love, admiration, and all other emotions and sensations that exist or have ever existed. It is not enough to know what these emotions feel like in a general way any more than it is enough to know what human bodies are like in a general way.

In the Qur'an, Allah's knowledge extends to every detail of existing things, no matter how insignificant: "Yes, by my Lord, it will surely come to you. [Allah is] the Knower of the unseen. Not absent from Him is an atom's weight within the heavens or within the earth or [what is] smaller than that or greater, except that it is in a clear register."[4] This includes what is inside human minds: "And surely your Lord knows what their breasts conceal and what they declare.[5] "And We have already created man and know what his soul whispers to him, and We are closer to him than [his] jugular vein."[6]

In the Hebrew Scriptures, David says to Solomon, "And you, my son Solomon, know the God of your father, and serve him with single mind and willing heart; for the Lord searches every mind, and understands every plan and thought" (1 Chron. 28:9, NRSV). Both this verse and the verses from the Qur'an imply that God's knowledge of human minds is like very close perception, with little distance between God's mind and our own. Close perception is one model of omnisubjectivity that we will look at in Chapter 3. Notice that in both the Hebrew scriptures and in the Qur'an, the difference between God as knowing subject and our minds as individual objects is preserved. There is *some* distance between God's mind and our minds, however slight.

Philosophers in the monotheistic traditions are firm on the comprehensiveness of God's knowledge down to every detail. Aquinas

---

[4] Surat An-Nami. Qur'an C:34, V:3. https://legacy.quran.com/34/3.
[5] Surat An-Nami. Qur'an C:27, V:74. https://legacy.quran.com/27/74.
[6] Surat Qaf. Qur'an C:50, V:16. https://legacy.quran.com/50/16.

adopted the position of Ibn Sina (Avicenna) that complete knowledge of the cause gives God complete knowledge of everything that follows from the cause, and he maintained that things would not even exist were it not for God's knowledge of them as their ultimate cause (*ST* I q. 14 a. 8). Everything exists and continues in existence because God knows it. That includes every act of knowing and the mode in which we know. If the first-person perspective is a mode of knowing, as I have argued, it follows that we know from our first-person perspective because God is the first cause of this perspective. God's knowledge must include knowledge of our subjective experiences not only because our subjective states are part of everything and God knows everything, but because God is the ultimate cause of those states and keeps them in existence.[7]

In Hinduism, the Self (*Atman*) is omniscient, but is beyond the distinction between knower and known. The beginning of the Kena Upanishad asks:

Who makes my mind think?
Who fills my body with vitality?
Who causes my tongue to speak? Who is that
Invisible one who sees through my eyes
And hears through my ears? (Kena Upanishad 1)

The answer is that it is the Self:

The Self is the ear of the ear,
The eye of the eye, the mind of the mind,
The word of words, and the life of life. (Kena Upanishad 2)

---

[7] I am indebted to Bernhard Blankenhorn, O. P. (2016) for his reply to my 2016 omnisubjectivity paper. Blankenhorn stresses the Thomistic idea that God is present in all things as their cause (2016, 451). Blankenhorn is right that that strengthens the argument for God's omnisubjectivity from omniscience.

One way to interpret this passage and others in the Upanishads is that the Self sees through my eyes because it is the consciousness that moves the universe. But I don't see how that can be right because consciousness is not conscious for the same reason that sight does not see and hearing does not hear. Consciousness requires a bearer.[8] So my interpretation is that the Self is the being whose consciousness permeates the universe and possesses universal consciousness. My seeing and feeling are the seeing and feeling of the Self. The Self is omnisubjective, and that is because there is only one Self that exists in me and in every other conscious being. What Westerners generally do not like about this idea is that there is no distance at all between the Self and the individual human mind. But pantheism and panentheism are also part of the Western tradition, and I will look at that approach further in Chapter 3.

Ever since the advent of the modern idea of a proposition—the putative abstract entity that has truth value—it has been common to define omniscience as the property of knowing the truth value of all propositions.[9] I have said that the cognitive grasp of reality might not be mediated through propositions, and exhaustive knowledge of propositions is insufficient for grasping the realm of subjectivity. Let me return to that point.

Marcel Sarot (1991) argues in an interesting paper about omniscience and experience that even the most comprehensive series of propositions cannot capture exactly how pain feels, and I would add that it certainly cannot capture exactly how any given instance of pain feels. In Chapter 1 I made the same claim about many other feelings, particularly feelings elicited by music or depicted in art, many of which have no names, or at least, no precise names.

[8] Frege makes a remark like this in his article "The Thought: A Logical Inquiry" (Frege 1956).
[9] The idea of defining omniscience as knowledge of the truth value of all propositions goes back at least to the 1970s (Swinburne 1977; Davis 1979). It was also used by Freddoso (1984), Kvanvig (1986), Wierenga (1989), and myself (Zagzebski 1991). The idea that omniscience is closer to cognitive perfection appears in Kvanvig (1990).

Propositions are usually thought to be expressed in language that packs reality into words put together into a sentential structure. Language has enormous power and scope, but it is hubris to think that its power extends to all of reality except in the most general way. Recall Aquinas's reply to the position that knowing universals is sufficient for knowing particulars. That might seem at first glance to be nothing more than a contribution to an arcane medieval dispute with no relevance to contemporary concerns, but I think that it is highly relevant because it is the same as the issue of the relationship between the general and the particular. Most of language is general, and we use general terms for subjective states. Squeezing a particular part of reality under a general term like "pain" misses what makes one pain different from every other. This point applies to physical nature also, but it is most obvious in the case of subjective states. Reality extends beyond what can be mapped onto natural language. If propositions are abstract entities expressible in language, reality extends beyond what corresponds to propositions. If there are propositions that are not expressible in natural language, then, as I mentioned in the last chapter, they become mysterious and lose much of their usefulness in aiding our understanding. But aside from the deficiencies of language, if there is something fundamentally unique about the first-person perspective, it is inexplicable how it can correspond to any abstract object.

Anthony Kenny (1979) defends the Wittgensteinian view that all our conscious states are communicable, and that anything that is not communicable cannot be known. If it is communicable, it can be expressed propositionally. Kenny says, "'Only I can know my sensation' means either that others cannot *know* that I am (e.g.) in pain; or that others cannot *feel* my pain. If it means the former, then it is obviously false. . . . If it means the latter then it is true but trivial, and there is no question of knowledge here" (1979, 111). I have two responses to this argument. One is to repeat what I said above that whenever someone else knows that I am in pain, they do not know exactly what I am feeling, only that it is similar enough to feelings of pain that they have had themselves to permit the feeling to come under the same general term "pain." Second, to repeat my response to the story of Mary in the last chapter, it does not matter whether awareness of what pain feels like counts as knowledge. The point is that there is a difference between knowing that someone is in pain, and knowing pain through experiencing it, or knowing that something is red and knowing what it is like to see red through seeing it. As long as that difference exists, it is something that needs to be grasped by a being who is cognitively perfect. It does not help to define "knowledge" in a way that removes the grasp of first-person sensations and feelings from the category of knowledge. Any differences in the created universe must be grasped by a being who grasps all particulars and is the ultimate cause of their existence. Each of us grasps what it is like to be in the conscious states we are in right now, and those states are parts of the created world. If God does not grasp those states and distinguish them from each other, God is not cognitively perfect.

Sarot concludes that in order to be omniscient, God does not need to share all the feelings of his creatures, but he must have undergone at least some experiences himself. Sarot says that a being who has had only a limited number of experiences may completely know the full range of creaturely experiences. That is because God can extrapolate from his limited experience. For instance, if he experienced only a mild pain, he can imagine what a stronger pain feels like (1991, 96). I do not find this answer satisfactory because I accept Aquinas's position that God grasps directly all the particulars of his creation, and nothing can even exist without his constant knowledge of it. So, I think that Sarot's position is too weak in one way, but too strong in another. It is too weak in that Sarot does not believe that an omniscient God must grasp each and every subjective state of each creature. I think it is too strong because Sarot believes God must actually *have* creaturely experiences in order to be omniscient. That is an empiricist principle that I will discuss in the next chapter. I will argue that it is false because it interprets God's imaginative grasp of our subjective states on too close an analogy with the human imagination.

There is only one world, but there is more than way to grasp or apprehend that world. Subjectivity is first-person awareness. Mary is aware of what red looks like when she leaves her uncolored room, and that is different from knowing all the propositional facts about red, which she knew before she opened the door. I have argued that Mary's mode of apprehension of red is itself part of the one world we all live in. Her state of apprehension is not something distinct from the world. A cognitively perfect God must, therefore, be aware of Mary's state of apprehension. God must fully and accurately grasp each creaturely state, not just the object of each creaturely state. God is not the omniscient being of the great monotheistic religions unless he is omnisubjective.

2.3. Omnipresence

A second traditional attribute of God is omnipresence, or the property of being everywhere. Omnipresence ties God intimately to the creation, so it is opposed to the position that God is solely a transcendent being. John W. Cooper (2006) relates omnipresence to divine immanence in a way that I find helpful: "God's immanence means that all spaces, times, entities, and events in creation are immediately present to him and he to them as their sustainer. God is omnipresent" (2006, 329). But the God of classical theism is also a transcendent being, and it is puzzling to see how a transcendent God can be immanent in the created world. Omnipresence is one aspect of that puzzle. The question "How can a transcendent God exist in all places?" is parallel to the question "How can a transcendent God exist at all times?" Most classical theists deny that God can literally be in space,[10] although many affirm that God can literally be

---

[10] For a contrary view, see Hud Hudson (2009) for an influential argument that God is actually located at every region of space.

in time. The contrast in the treatment of the two questions is interesting, but I will not pursue that point. If God transcends space and time, how can God be *in* events in space and time? I believe that the answer to that question entails omnisubjectivity.

Omnipresence is a central attribute of God in Hinduism. In the Vedas, Brahman exists beyond creation but is intrinsic to it because Brahman's consciousness is projected into the material universe. The beginning of the Isha Upanishad declares that the whole universe is inhabited by the Lord of the universe, proclaiming "The Lord is enshrined in the heart of all. The Lord is the supreme Reality." A few verses later it reads:

> In dark night live those for whom the Lord
> Is transcendent only; in night darker still,
> For whom he is immanent only.
> But those for whom he is transcendent
> And immanent cross the sea of death
> With the immanent and enter into
> Immortality with the transcendent.
> So have we heard from the wise. (Isha 12–14)

In Judaism and Christianity, as in the Upanishads, the omnipresence of God is associated with the belief that God is the master of the universe and nothing escapes his eye:

> Can a man hide in secret,
> Without my seeing him? Says the Lord.
> Do I not fill
> Both heaven and earth? Says the Lord. (Jer. 23:24, NAB)

And the psalmist says:

> Where can I go from your spirit?
> O where can I flee from your presence?

> If I ascend to heaven, you are there;
> If I make my bed in Sheol, you are there.
> If I take the wings of the morning
> and settle at the farthest limits of the sea,
> even there your hand shall lead me,
> and your right hand shall hold me fast. (Ps. 139: 7–10, NRSV)

The Qur'an also emphasizes the omnipresence of God: "And He is with you wherever you are";[11] and "So wherever you [might] turn, there is the Face of Allah."[12]

Ordinary believers take for granted that God is omnipresent and rarely worry about the compatibility of omnipresence with the belief that God is beyond the spatiotemporal world, but Aquinas states the problem succinctly in an objection to omnipresence: "It seems that God is not everywhere. For to be everywhere means to be in every place. But to be in every place does not belong to God, to Whom it does not belong to be in place at all; for incorporeal things, as Boethius says, are not in a place. Therefore, God is not everywhere" (ST I q. 8 a. 2 obj 1).

Aquinas's answer to the objection reduces the omnipresence of God to other attributes. He says that God is in all things in three ways: by his power, since all things are subject to his power; by the presence of his knowledge, since "all things are bare and open to his eyes"; and by his essence, because he is present to all as the cause of their being (ST I, q. 8, a. 3). Notice that Aquinas interprets omnipresence in a way that eliminates any reference to space per se. Omnipresence applies to all things in the created world, whether material or immaterial, spatial or nonspatial. There is nothing special about spatial objects.

Anselm's solution to the problem of omnipresence goes directly to the issue of what it means to be present. He denies that being

---

[11] Surat Al-Hadid. Qur'an C: 57. V:4. https://legacy.quran.com/57/4.
[12] Surat Al-Baquara. Qur'an C:2 V:115. https://legacy.quran.com/2/115.

present requires being extended in space or being contained by some portion of space, the way a chair is contained by the room in which it is located and spread out on the floor beneath it. God has no parts and does not take up space, yet God is wholly "present" in each part of the created world (*Monologion* 20). This is a very plausible position. It means that there is nothing distinctive about God's presence in spatial beings rather than nonspatial beings. Anselm accepts that implication explicitly when he says, "The supreme nature exists in everything that exists, just as much as it exists in every place. It is not contained, but contains all, by permeating all. This we know. Why not say, then, that it is 'everywhere' (meaning in everything that exists) rather than 'in every place'" (*Monologion* 23).

For both Aquinas and Anselm, then, the explanation of how a spatial being can be present at all points of space applies to the nonspatial part of the creation as well as to the spatial world. If God cannot be "in" a physical place the way a coffee cup is in the cupboard, any sense in which God *can* be in a physical place applies to nonphysical parts of the creation. God is present in everything, including our own minds.

Are our subjective states in space? If subjective states are in space, presumably located where our bodies are located, then omnipresence entails omnisubjectivity for the same reason that it entails that God is wherever your body is. If instead, our subjective states do not have a spatial location, and omnipresence means "in everything that exists," as Anselm proposes, then again, omnipresence entails omnisubjectivity. Whether or not our subjective states are in space, God is in them.

The metaphysical connection between God and the spatial world is perplexing, and some contemporary philosophers have offered theories about that connection. Richard Swinburne (1977) proposes that God is related to the created world analogously to the way an immaterial human soul is related to her body (1977, 104–106). Swinburne suggests that God knows and controls all things directly, just as each of us controls her body, and he suggests that this is what has traditionally been meant by omnipresence (1977, 106). It is intriguing that Plato proposes something similar in the *Timaeus* where God makes a world-soul with the material world as its body:

> Such was the whole plan of the eternal God about the god that was to be; he made it smooth and even, having a surface in every direction equidistant from the center, a body entire and perfect, and formed out of perfect bodies. And in the center he put the soul, which he diffused throughout the body, making it also to be the exterior environment of it, and he made the universe a circle moving in a circle, one and solitary, yet by its excellence able to converse with itself, and needing no other friendship or acquaintance. Having these purposes in view he created the world a blessed god. (1977, 34b; trans. Benjamin Jowett)

Versions of Plato's idea have been repeated in Western thought, usually without the delightful imagery. In the mid-twentieth century, Charles Hartshorne (1941, 185) defended the idea that omnipresence entails that the world literally is God's body. He called his view panentheism, in contrast to pantheism, or the view that God and the universe are ontologically identical. Hartshorne's theology is not classical theism, and many Christian philosophers will be unwilling to go so far as to say that the created universe is contained within God. But Hartshorne and others who accept panentheism have noticed something that is difficult to deny. The classical approach to explaining omnipresence is to reinterpret it as either reducible to other attributes, as Aquinas does in reducing it to God's power, knowledge, and causal activity, or to make omnipresence the same thing as God's immanence, as Anselm does in saying that omnipresence just means "in everything." But what does it mean to be "in" your pain? Is it even possible? The implications of omnipresence force us to confront the relationship between the transcendence and the immanence of God, and the relationship between the consciousness of one individual and the consciousness of the being who is the creator of earthly consciousness. Omnipresence has the consequence that God *should* be omnisubjective. The harder part is showing how it is possible.

Omnipresence has another aspect suggested by Aquinas's claim that to God, all things are "bare and open to his eyes." If God not only knows that you are anxious, but God is present in your anxiety, that raises the possibility that you and God are present to each other. Eleonore Stump (2013) argues that omnipresence requires mutual personal presence in which two persons are aware of each other and they are aware of their mutual awareness: "In order for God to be present at every place, as Christianity claims God is, it also needs to be the case that, for any person at any place who is able and willing to share attention with God, God is available to share attention with that person" (2013, 36).

Stump (2010) has movingly defended the presence of one person to another as a condition for the union of love. God's love for his creatures requires intimate presence, not just the distant kind of presence in which one being has power over another or is the cause of the other's being. The possibility of intimate relationships between human persons and God is an important part of Christian teaching. I will return to that issue in discussing the infusion of the Holy Spirit in Chapter 6.

2.4. The Practices of Prayer

Analytic philosophers of religion are used to analyzing religious writing and teaching as sets of propositions expressed in the third person, and they do that even when the work is actually written in the second person, addressed to God. Discussions of St. Anselm are a good example. His famous ontological argument for the existence of God in the *Proslogion* is spoken to God. Anselm asks God to give understanding to his faith, and he addresses God as "you" throughout his reflections. But there is a big difference be-tween thinking about the existence of God to yourself and others who care to discuss your thoughts, and addressing your thoughts to God himself, asking for inspiration, and continuously aware of the presence of God while writing sentences that will be excerpted by commentators a thousand years later. It is understandable that commentators sometimes ignore Anselm's relationship to God since they might think that it is none of their business, but doing so distorts Anselm's subjectivity and its place in some of the most pro-found philosophical work.

Prayer is an intrinsic feature of the great monotheistic religions. Usually, people believe that God hears them, but many people pray even when they have no confidence that there is a God who listens and cares. Hope is sometimes enough. Amber Griffioen (2021) argues that prayer is an exercise of the religious imagination that can make belief almost irrelevant. She says that we want a God who is relatable, with whom we can connect, and the religious imagina-tion permits the subject to reach out toward the divine in second-person address. The person who prays can be committed to the rituals, norms, concepts, and propositions of the religious life, but may not fully believe those propositions, perhaps because she does not fully understand them. So, people who pray do not necessarily believe that God is listening, but they at least hope or imagine that God is listening, and is listening as a person listens, not the way a radio telescope listens to signals from distant space.

Prayer can take great effort, even when it is most needed, and perhaps especially when it is most needed. Georges Bernanos' novel, *Diary of a Country Priest*, relates the daily thoughts and tribulations of a young priest whose spiritual growth deepens as his physical health is slowly destroyed by cancer. At one of his lowest moments, he writes,

Another horrible night, sleep interspersed with evil dreams. It was raining so hard that I couldn't venture into church. Never have I made such efforts to pray, at first calmly and steadily, then with a kind of savage, concentrated violence, till at last, having struggled back into calm with a huge effort, I persisted, almost desperately (desperately! How horrible it sounds!) in a sheer transport of will which set me shuddering with anguish. Yet— nothing. (1936, 103)

Then, in the next line, he writes the most often quoted words of Bernanos: "I know . . . that the wish to pray is a prayer in itself, that God can ask no more than that of us" (1936, 103). Bernanos's priest is fictional, but like many people in the real world, he understands prayer as something that has already happened with the intention, the desire, which God clearly sees in his consciousness. The country priest has strong faith but sometimes cannot pray. The person described by Griffioen does not have strong faith, but can still pray. Their states of mind and heart and conviction are quite different, but they both direct their conscious state to a listener.

Once I was asked by a Christian philosopher if I pray to a certain member of the Trinity. I was taken aback because often I do not have any member of the Trinity in mind, which might indicate confusion on my part. Is it necessary to be clear about the person to whom one is praying? Later I will offer my conjecture on the relationship among the persons of the Trinity, proposing that they have three distinct subjectivities. I do not know how that would affect the practices of prayer, but I think that we can say at a minimum that common practices of prayer within all three of the great monotheistic religions deriving from Abraham assume that God is aware of our prayers. Catholics also pray to the saints. Aquinas's explanation was that saints can hear prayers by seeing in the divine essence what God grants for the purpose of aiding us in our salvation (*ST* Supplement q. 72. a.1). God is the principal recipient of our prayers even when the saints are intermediaries, and praying to the saints implies that God hears the saints. It is interesting that Aquinas makes God's essence the medium of awareness for the saints, and that is presumably because he also thinks that God is aware of our prayers through his essence.

There are many references to prayer in the Bible and the Qur'an that imply that God hears our prayers. For example, the Lord and Moses speak back and forth after the Israelites arrive in Palestine and the people threaten a revolt against Moses and Aaron. Then Moses asks, "Pardon, then, the wickedness of this people in keeping with your great kindness, even as you have forgiven them from Egypt until now." The Lord replies, "I pardon them as you have asked" (NAB Num. 14:19–20).

In the New Testament, Jesus teaches us to pray directly to the Father in the Lord's prayer (Matt. 6:9–13), and Jesus prays many times in seclusion. The Gospels of Matthew, Mark, and Luke tell us that he prays in the Garden of Gethsemane right before his passion and death (Matt 26:39; Mark 14:32–36; Luke 22:39–42), and the seventeenth chapter of John's Gospel is entirely composed of the prayers of Jesus before he goes to the garden and is arrested.

> As you, Father, are in me and I am in you, may they also be in us, so that the world may believe that you have sent me. The glory that you have given me I have given them, so that they may be one, as we are one. I in them and you in me, that they may be completely one, so that the world may know that you have sent me and have loved them even as you have loved me. (John 17:21–23, NRSV)

These words not only imply that Jesus believes that the Father hears him, but they imply intersubjectivity in the Father's relationship to Jesus.

The Qur'an is clear that individual persons may speak to God in prayer: "And when My servants ask you, [O Muhammed], concerning Me—indeed I am near. I respond to the invocation of the supplicant when he calls upon Me. So let them respond to me [by obedience] and believe in Me that they may be [rightly] guided.[13]

In addition to private prayer, Judaism, Christianity, and Islam have established cycles of ritual prayer that build a community of faith. These prayers are spoken and sung aloud in liturgies, and the central place of liturgy in religious practice makes it clear that prayer is not limited to a single individual's address to God.[14] Liturgical prayer is said aloud for the sake of the community, not for the sake of God. Spoken words are common, but are they necessary? Are even unspoken words necessary? In Catholic theology, prayer is defined as raising one's mind and heart to God.[15] One thing that is interesting about that definition is that it does not refer to words. Another curious feature is that it focuses on the human side of prayer and is silent about the recipient.

The philosophical literature on prayer is sparse, and what little there is usually focuses on issues about petitionary prayer. For instance, if God does not change, prayer cannot make him change, and if God is providential, there seems to be no need to pray anyway. But I am not focusing on any issues about petitionary prayer in particular. The issue I am raising is how we understand what is going on between us and God when we pray any kind of prayer. It could be a prayer of praise, of thanksgiving, of contrition, a request, or just a coming together with God.

If God can hear prayers, then surely, he can hear the words that are unspoken. As the psalmist says, "Even before a word is on my tongue, O Lord, you know it completely" (Psalm 139: 4 NRSV). And if God can hear unspoken words, what about images in our minds such as images of the Passion? Many meditative practices

[13] Surat Al-Baqarah. Qur'an 2:186. https://legacy.quran.com/2/186.

[14] For a good book-length treatment of the importance of ritual in religious practice, see Cuneo (2016). The topic of liturgy has been neglected in philosophy, and Cuneo gives a wide-ranging defense of the ways in which the study of liturgy is rewarding for the philosopher and the theologian.

[15] See *Catechism of the Catholic Church*, 2nd edition (1995, 2559, 2590). The wording of the definition is taken from St. John Damascene in the eighth century.

begin with images, and in more advanced states of contemplation the images disappear, and the person feels herself or himself to be in the presence of God with neither words nor images. Is God aware of that person's state? Surely that is no more difficult for God than hearing the unspoken words mentioned by the psalmist. In both cases God would have to be "in our head" to be aware of our mental state. But if he can be aware of words we are thinking, why not images we are having and feelings we are feeling?

What I have said about practices of prayer does not require the full attribute of omnisubjectivity because it does not require that God is intimately acquainted with the first-person perspective of beings who do not pray. But it requires at least the attribute of grasping the first-person perspective of all human beings who have ever lived and have ever prayed, or who will ever live and will ever pray. However, I think that our practices of prayer do not assume that God becomes aware of our conscious life only at the moment of the prayer. How could we address God in prayer unless God was already aware of what was happening in our consciousness? Our practices assume that God is directly acquainted with the conscious states of any being who can pray, whether or not that being actually prays. That would require the attribute of grasping the conscious states of all human beings from their own perspective. It would not apply to nonhuman conscious animals, animals who cannot pray. But if you accept such an attribute, it is but a small step to accepting the full attribute of omnisubjectivity. Surely a being who enters into the consciousness of a human enters into the consciousness of all creatures with consciousness. If he can do it for one, he can do it for all. The harder question is whether he can do it for any.

2.5. Divine Love

The arguments for omnisubjectivity from the philosophical tradition are strong. I have argued that both God's omniscience and

God's omnipresence entail omnisubjectivity, and it is supported by the scriptures of Judaism, Christianity, and Islam. Omnisubjectivity also extends deep into religious practice in the assumptions of ordinary believers about personal and communal prayer. But I would like to conclude this chapter with brief remarks about two other properties of God that strongly suggest omnisubjectivity: divine love and divine justice.

One of the most striking and moving passages in the New Testament affirms the unimaginable love God has for us: "Yes, God so loved the world that he gave his only Son, that whoever believes in him may not die but may have eternal life" (John 3:16).[16] The love of God is repeated over and over with specific references to the teaching that God is our father, and we are his children: "The Spirit himself gives us witness with our spirit that we are children of God" (Romans 8:16). God's love is deep in the universe: "But anyone who does not love does not know God, for God is love" (1 John 4:8). The moral demand for us to love others is based on the fact that God has already loved us.

Islam and Hinduism also refer to the love of God. One of the ninety-nine names of Allah is *Al-Wadoud* (the All-Loving). In *The Bhagavad Gita*, Lord Krishna says, "I am the source of all the joy, all the love, all the wisdom, and all the beauty within you" (Easwaran 2020, 118). The Shvetashvatara Upanishad says:

> In the depths of meditation, sages
> Saw within themselves the Lord of Love,
> Who dwells in the heart of every creature.
> Deep in the hearts of all he dwells, hidden
> Behind the gunas of law, energy,
> And inertia. He is One. He it is
> Who rules over time, space, and causality.
> (Shvetashvatara Upanishad 1.3)

---

[16] Translations in this paragraph are from the New American Bible (NAB).

It is interesting that there is a connection between being all-knowing and all-loving in the world religions. The logical order is first knowing, then loving. In Christianity this order is deep in the theology of the Trinity. The Father's grasp of himself begets the Word, which is the Son. Aquinas argues that the Son proceeds from the Father and his proper name is Word (*ST* I q. 34). "Word" in God signifies what proceeds from the knowledge of the one conceiving (*ST* I q. 34 a. 1 corpus), so the Son proceeds from the Father's knowledge of himself (*ST* I q. 34 a.1 corpus). The Holy Spirit proceeds from the Father and the Son's love of each other and his proper name is Love (*ST* I q. 36, 37). Aquinas says, "the Son proceeds by the way of the intellect as Word, and the Holy Spirit by way of the will as Love. Now love must proceed from a word. For we do not love anything unless we apprehend it by a mental conception" (*ST* I q. 36 a. 2 corpus).

I believe that the God of Christianity loves each of us as irreplaceable individuals, not simply as instances of human nature. I have argued in other places (2000, 2016b) that the value of irreplaceability cannot be grounded in anything shareable such as our rationality, and I propose that it is grounded in the unique subjectivity of each person. In the last chapter, I briefly mentioned the historical background of the connection between subjectivity and individual uniqueness. If I am right that subjectivity is the ground of our irreplaceability, then God must grasp the subjectivity of each of us. To be fully and deeply loved necessitates being fully and deeply known as irreplaceable persons. What each of us goes through in living our lives day to day is an intrinsic part of who we are. We appreciate other persons who are able to share in our experiences and understand us partly through understanding those experiences as we see them, and we think that the deepest human love is based on the deepest knowledge of our inner being. Surely God does more perfectly what ordinary humans can do for each other.

For millennia, love has been expressed, discussed, analyzed, and portrayed in virtually every part of human culture: art, literature, philosophy, theology, psychology, and science. A common theme and an important one is that an essential component of love is desire for union with the loved one. That makes love more than benevolence, or the desire for the well-being of another. We can have benevolent feelings and motives toward others without paying a great deal of attention to them, but love is different. People who love each other want to share their lives as intimately as possible without one of them becoming submerged in the ego of the other. We do not want to *be* the other, but we want to be united in a blend of minds and emotions that would not be possible without a comprehension of the mind and emotions of each other. I think that intersubjective union is more than a precondition for love; it is a component of loving itself. In human men and women intersubjective union is aided by physical union, but different kinds of beings enjoy different forms of union, and God can be united with any being with subjectivity.

The ideal of love I have described might seem inappropriate and even impossible if the lover is God and the loved one is a creature. The distance between divine and creaturely nature is infinite and anything that would count as intersubjective harmony would not be equally balanced—half one subjective life, and half the other. I have sometimes heard people say that you cannot love anybody who is not your equal, but surely that is false. People often love their dog or their cat or their horse or their pig. The human's subjectivity obviously includes much more than that of the pet. The pet finds much of what makes us human mysterious, and we cannot always comprehend what makes our pets feel the way they do, but exchanges of subjectivity between species is easy, and communication is usually of subjective states, not objective facts. If subjectivity pervades the universe from God down to creatures like fish and octopuses, we would expect the love of God for his creation to reach at least as far down as all the subjectivity he created.

Is it possible to love wholly without perfect knowledge? There is a sense in which we can love God wholly without knowing God wholly. Aquinas addresses this problem: "It would seem that God cannot be loved wholly. For love follows knowledge. Now God cannot be wholly known by us since this would imply comprehension of Him. Therefore, He cannot be wholly loved by us" (*ST* II-II q. 17 a. 6 obj. 1). As you would expect, Aquinas makes a distinction. His answer is that no creature can love God infinitely, but human creatures can still love God with all their might, and in that sense, they can love God wholly (*ST* II-II q. 17. a. 6 corpus). So, for creatures, loving wholly does not presuppose knowing wholly. But it is different for God who loves us because he has created our goodness (*ST* II-II q. 20. a. 2, corpus) and he has known us from all eternity in our "proper" (particular) nature (*ST* II-II reply obj 2).

Notice that for Aquinas, as for the ancient Greeks, love is directed toward the good, and that implies that whatever there is in us that is not good is not worthy of love. But the doctrine of the Redemption and the healing of sin is a doctrine of the love God has for us in spite of the sinfulness of human beings, so divine love cannot be directed only toward the good in human persons. In fact, the good in human persons is there because of God. But there is another way in which Aquinas's conception of divine love disregards a central feature of love. In focusing on the good, Aquinas ignores the particularity of the loved one. This problem can be found as far back as Plato's *Symposium*, where Socrates argues in his speech on love that love is directed toward the Form Beauty or the Good. Each individual physically or spiritually beautiful person is loved for the way they participate in the Good itself, and he defines love as the desire for the perpetual possession of the Good (*Symposium* 206 A 9). It has been observed by others that Socrates does not appreciate the love of persons for their individuality,[17] but whether he appreciates it or

---

[17] See Martha Nussbaum (2001, 165–199) on the speech of Alcibiades in the *Symposium*. Nussbaum argues that unlike Socrates, Alcibiades knows what it is to love an individual person, not the imitation of a Platonic Form in a person. But it is worth noticing that Plato wrote the speech of Alcibiades as well as the speech of Socrates.

not, we do, and I submit that persons are loved for their individual uniqueness, and that is rooted in their subjectivity.

After the discovery of subjectivity in the West, it took more centuries for philosophers and ordinary people to adopt the belief that the irreplaceable value of human beings is based on their unique subjectivity. So, the defense I have proposed for omnisubjectivity from the love of God is based on reading scripture passages and medieval philosophy through the eyes of a metaphysical category that did not exist when those works were written. But the idea of subjectivity is not going away, nor would we want it to. I think that it is up to us to combine insights from the sacred writings of the past and the best philosophy we have inherited from the premodern period with the most important modern discoveries. It is in that spirit that I say that the love of God for us requires the most thorough grasp of our subjectivity.

2.6. Divine Justice

I would like to conclude with one more reason to think that God must be omnisubjective. Omnisubjectivity is a requirement of perfect justice. There are passages in both the Old and the New Testaments that imply that God renders justice on the basis of knowing everything in the human heart: "I the Lord test the mind and search the heart, to give to all according to their ways, according to the fruit of their doings" (Jer. 17:10, NRSV). And St. Paul writes: "Indeed, the word of God is living and active, sharper than any two-edged sword, piercing until it divides soul from spirit, joints from marrow; it is able to judge the thoughts and intentions of the heart. And before him no creature is hidden, but all are naked and laid bare to the eyes of the one to whom we must render an account" (Heb. 4:12–13, NRSV).

In the Upanishads there is no divine judge at death who scrutinizes a person's past inner and outer life, but one's past life, and especially the deepest desires of that life, determine the life that follows: "A person is what his deep desire is. It is our deepest desire in this life that shapes the life to come" (Chandogya Upanishad III 14.1). The cycle of rebirth is described in the Shvetashvatara Upanishad:

> The Self takes on a body with desires,
> Attachments, and delusions, and is
> Born again and again in new bodies
> To work out the karma of former lives.
> The embodied self assumes many forms,
> Heavy or light, according to its needs
> For growth and the deeds of previous lives.
> This evolution is a divine law. (Shvetashvatara Upanishad 5. 11–12)

The idea that there is cosmic justice that depends upon what goes on in an individual person's mind as much as or even more than that person's deeds is widespread in world religions. In some religions justice in the universe is an impersonal force of cause and effect like karma. In the Abrahamic religions justice in the universe is administered by a divine judge who governs the universe and settles all accounts on a Day of Judgment. It is assumed that the good and evil of human deeds arise from the good and evil in the human heart. To conform our deeds to the good we must make our hearts pure.

> Probe me, O God, and know my heart;
>   try me and know my thoughts;
> See if my way is crooked,
>   and lead me in the way of old. (Ps. 139, 23–24, NAB)

I interpret that to mean that the divine judge grasps the subjectivity of each individual person. Our subjectivity is the root of who we are. The nuances of our every thought, the moods that affect our strength of will, the history of experiences that aid or inhibit the development of virtue, the confusion in our desires—all of that is significant to the Judge who judges us for who we are. If we are judged for who we are in the deepest way, we are judged for our subjective states as they combine, push and pull us, and generate our distinctive path over a lifetime.

It is understandable that many of us are frightened by the idea that we cannot escape ultimate judgment. There is too much in our lives that we would rather see disappear from God's watchful eye. But Christianity teaches that forgiveness is always within reach. I think of forgiveness as the combination of justice and love. Like love, forgiveness is interpersonal. God can forgive without telling us, but God desires reconciliation with us, and reconciliation is interpersonal and is based on an accurate grasp of every detail of our sins. God's love and God's justice separately imply a thorough grasp of our subjective states, but the blend of the two produces complex states of intersubjective consciousness like mercy and reconciliation, and those states remove the sting of judgment.

God's justice is a component of his providential governance of the world. We turn to God for help in managing our feelings and the direction of our lives. We know that there is somebody who knows us thoroughly, even better than we know ourselves, and whose guidance and love helps us to be our better selves. That being must have a perfect grasp of our subjectivity. God can make the flow of our subjective states a component of his providential narrative, the big story of the world. I will return to the big story at the end of this essay.

The conditions necessary for divine justice, like the conditions implied in practices of prayer, do not require the full attribute of omnisubjectivity. I assume that God does not judge or need to forgive nonhuman animals based on the state of their subjective consciousness. But what I said about prayer applies in the case of divine judgment. A power necessary for divine–human interaction is the same power God can exercise in grasping the animal mind. True, God does not need to grasp the subjectivity of animals for the purpose of judging them,[18] but judging is a component of providential governance, and that applies to animals as well as to human beings. Divine providence extends to every living creature in every aspect of their being. There is no reason to think that a providential God would limit his power of grasping subjectivity to humans.

Readers will no doubt notice that the arguments I have given for divine omnisubjectivity in this chapter are interconnected, and that is because the attributes of God and their place in religious practice are interconnected. God is omniscient, not just because he knows the truth value of all propositions, but because he is intimately present to everything that goes on in the world he created. His presence extends to what is going on in our minds, and that is why God hears our prayers. That presence also allows God to deliver just judgments based on knowing all our hidden motives, feelings, temptations, rational or irrational beliefs, strengths and weaknesses, dreams and fears, psychic blocks, neuroses, and anything else that could be mitigating or aggravating circumstances relevant to our behavior. God's presence means that God's love is directed toward us as we really are. Omnisubjectivity makes possible God's complete knowledge, presence, justice, and love. It explains how the union of love between God and us is possible, and it explains how God hears our unspoken prayers.

I find omnisubjectivity intellectually fascinating and emotionally comforting. It means that we can always share our joy and we are never alone in our suffering. In quiet moments we can reflect about the nature of God and what an omnisubjective God would be like. But we need to feel confident that it is a possible attribute.

---

[18] An interesting exception to the prevailing view that animals are not judged by God is the position of Trent Dougherty (2014, ch. 8) who proposes that there are animal saints.

3

How God Can Be Omnisubjective

3.1. Introduction

Divine omnisubjectivity is necessary if it is possible, but how is it possible? If it is impossible but is entailed by omniscience and omnipresence, then omniscience and omnipresence are impossible, and common practices of prayer do not make sense. Patrick Grim (1985) has argued that God cannot know propositions expressed by sentences like "I made a mess in the market," and therefore, there is no omniscient God. Yujin Nagasawa (2008, 23–25) responds that we should think of divine omniscience in terms of epistemic power. If it is impossible for God to know what I know in knowing "I made the mess," it does not follow that God is not omniscient because it is not a lack of epistemic power in God to be unable to do the necessarily impossible. God cannot know what I know when I know that I am the one who made the mess for the same reason God cannot square a circle.[1]

If it is impossible for anyone but you to know your conscious states from your first-person viewpoint, Nagasawa's argument might save the day for the doctrine of omniscience. Possibly it can also save the day for the doctrine of omnipresence. It could be argued in the same vein that omnipresence does not entail being present where presence is impossible, and it is not possible for God to be present in your subjective states as you experience them for the same reason it is not possible for God to know what you know when you experience your states of consciousness.

[1] See Torre (2006) for another response to Patrick Grim.

Omnisubjectivity. Linda Trinkaus Zagzebski, Oxford University Press. © Oxford University Press 2023. DOI: 10.1093/oso/9780197682098.003.0003

I would not deny that if omnisubjectivity is impossible, omniscience and omnipresence can be defined in a way that is compatible with God's lack of knowledge and presence in our subjective states, but my arguments in the last chapter were intended to show not only that omnisubjectivity is entailed by traditional definitions of omniscience and omnipresence, but that it is entailed by cognitive perfection. Furthermore, we *want* God to be omnisubjective. Our practices of prayer imply that God grasps our subjective states, and the way we think of God's justice and love also imply it. If we want God to know our subjective states, we must hope that omnisubjectivity is possible. I will argue in this chapter that it is.

In Chapter 1 I argued that subjectivity is something in addition to what exists in the objectively describable world. When Mary leaves her uncolored room and sees in color for the first time, her experience is something new that did not previously exist, and a being who knows everything must grasp the difference between that experience and Mary's previous experience. Even if Mary's experience is not a "thing" in an ontology of objects, there is a difference in her experience before and after she leaves the room. The difference is real, but arguably, it is only detectable inside Mary's mind. How is it possible for God to be in Mary's mind without being Mary? How is it possible for God to be in your mind without being you?

The same problem arises for omnipresence. When we talk about God being present at all points of space, people do not worry that there is no room for God in a place filled up with physical objects. They assume that God is a spirit who does not take up space. But it is different for your mental space because usually what we *mean* by your mental space is what is yours alone. If you and God are distinct individuals with minds that are not only distinct, but necessarily distinct, and if what makes your mind distinct is your subjective states, it seems to follow that all minds other than yours are necessarily blocked from your subjective states by the individuality of minds.

Suppose that it is not possible for anybody but you to literally feel your pain. Does that also mean that it is not possible for anybody but you to grasp the way your pain feels—the feeling itself, not just the fact that the pain exists? That depends upon the relationship between having a feeling and grasping that feeling perfectly. Suppose a feeling is grasped in the imagination. Is a perfect imaginative grasp of a feeling different from an actual feeling? How close to us can God get without invading our selfhood? In this chapter I will offer three models of omnisubjectivity and a metaphor. The first is the model of empathy. The second is the model of perception. The third is panentheism. The first two attempt to help us see the possibility of fully and accurately grasping a feeling or thought or intention without being the one who has it. The third model is one in which the creature who has the thought or feeling is part of God. I will then discuss the metaphor of light to help us imagine the possibility that creaturely consciousness is infused by divine consciousness while being ontologically distinct from God. I am offering more than one model because I want to propose options to theists who arrive at the idea of omnisubjectivity with different theological frameworks and antecedent views about the self.

I believe that analogies and metaphors can aid our metaphysical imaginations. We may think of the empathy model and the perceptual model as analogies in either the stronger medieval sense or in the weaker modern sense. Aquinas uses the term "analogy" differently than it is used in contemporary discourse. In discussing how we can apply terms to God, Aquinas says that a term can be used univocally, equivocally, or analogously. In an analogous use of a term, there is more than one meaning, but the meanings are connected. A term like "good" or "thinks" when applied to us is deficient relative to its application to God. God's goodness comes first and causes our goodness. We participate in the goodness of God. God is good in a prior sense of the term. Divine empathy and perception could be taken as analogies in that sense. However, I think that even analogies in the weaker modern sense can be helpful in aiding our understanding of the possibility of omnisubjectivity. We use analogies in the weaker sense to indicate a parallelism of structure or relations that allows us to infer more similarities between the two analogues. The theistic Argument from Design uses analogy in this sense, and the empathy and perceptual models might be taken as analogies in this sense. Panentheism is more than an analogy in either sense because it is a metaphysical theory in which God actually has our subjective states. The human mind is not separate from the mind of God.

The primary use of the word "in" is to indicate spatial relations, but there are multiple senses of the term. Different ways in which something can be in something else will come up repeatedly in this chapter. In the perceptual model, God is not quite in your mind; in the empathy model God is in your mind imaginatively. Neither model is spatial. In panentheism we are in God and God is in us because we are not really distinct from God. God could also be in us like light is in transparent objects. That image suggests that God can be in our conscious states without going as far as panentheism in maintaining that our states are parts of God.

It is interesting that Gottlob Frege thinks of the issue of this chapter when he compares the subjective experiences of two persons, and he immediately considers the possibility that our consciousness is part of the divine consciousness. He begins by saying that if the word "red" signifies an impression within my own consciousness, it is impossible to compare my sense impression with that of someone else.

It is so much of the essence of each of my ideas to be the content of my consciousness, that every idea of another person is, just as such, distinct from mine. But might it not be possible that my ideas, the entire content of my consciousness, might be at the same time the content of a more embracing, perhaps divine, consciousness? Only if I were myself part of the divine consciousness. But then would they really be my ideas, would I be their

bearer? This oversteps the limits of human understanding to such
an extent that one must leave its possibility out of account. In any
case it is impossible for us as men to compare another person's
ideas with our own. I pick the strawberry, I hold it between my
fingers. Now my companion sees it too, this very same strawberry; but each of us has his own idea. No other person has my
idea, but many people can see the same thing. No other person
has my pain. Someone can have sympathy for me but still my pain
always belongs to me and his sympathy to him. He does not have
my pain and I do not have his sympathy. (Frege 1956, 299–301)[2]

Although Frege does not say so, his observation about the separation of the subjective states of one person from those of someone
else conflicts with another very basic intuition about the world as
a whole: the intuition that everything in the world is connected.
Both theists and nontheists have this intuition. Physicalists take
for granted that the entire universe is a unity connected by physical
laws and processes. In fact, the belief that everything in the universe
is connected is so strong that physicalists consider it an advantage
of their theory if it explains that connection, and a disadvantage if
it cannot do so. Theists also assume that everything is connected. It
is connected in the mind of God who is the creator and governor of
the universe.[3] God has no trouble putting it all together. But if it can
all be put together, that means that the subjectivity of one person
is in some way connected to the subjectivity of another. But that
conflicts with the idea that subjectivity is what separates one mind
from another. Are minds connected or not?

---

[2] I thank Chad McIntosh for calling my attention to this passage many years ago. I am
also grateful for his review (McIntosh 2015) of my Aquinas Lecture at Marquette on
omnisubjectivity.
[3] Thomas Nagel (2010) says that it is a disadvantage of theism that it seems to bifurcate
nature and the supernatural. It is interesting that he assumes that the world as a whole
cannot be divided into two distinct parts.

Models and metaphors test the human imagination just as much as the idea that our minds are parts of God, the possibility that Frege briefly considers and rejects as beyond human understanding. I think that all these approaches push human understanding to its limits, perhaps beyond the limits, but I think that they are all worth serious consideration.

3.2. The Model of Total Empathy

My first model is empathy. In human empathy we grasp the conscious state of another person as if we were that person. At least, that is what we try to do, and we probably can succeed up to a point. When I empathize with my friend Pat's grief, I become aware of her grief and I acquire a representation of her emotion by going through a process of taking on her perspective—imagining what it would be like to be Pat in her situation as she sees it—for example, to have lost her father and to have her personal history with him. When I imagine what it would be like to be Pat, I do not imagine that I (LZ) am identical with Pat. Clearly, that does not make sense. Rather, I imagine that Pat is I. To do that I must imagine that I am not my actual self, but I am Pat instead.[4] That is to say, I imagine a different *I* than the one I have in my nonimaginary life. Imagining myself as Pat, I take on her grief in my imagination. My imaginary grief is not qualitatively identical to the grief Pat feels because human empathy is never a perfect copy. More importantly, my emotion is consciously representational, whereas Pat's emotion is not. Pat's emotion comes first and has nothing to do with me. My emotion is in my imagination and comes in response to hers. It loses its point if I discover that she does not have the emotion I thought she had.[5]

[4] David Velleman (2020, 215) makes the same point that imagining being another person is not imagining anything about one's actual self. We do not imagine identities of distinct persons.

[5] Empathy can be confused with emotional contagion, in which an emotion spreads through a crowd the way fire spreads through a building, sometimes leading to panic

My psychic state arises from my attempt at copying Pat's emotion as it exists from her first-person perspective, but my imaginative emotion also includes my own ego. *I* do not grieve over the death of Pat's father whom I have never met, but I imaginatively adopt a state of grieving as if I were Pat.

Sympathy is often treated as the same as empathy, but I believe that they are different, and their differences affect the model I am describing.[6] I think of sympathy as fellow feeling, the positive feeling of affinity with others that leads us to wish them well. We can empathize without sympathizing. We sometimes empathize in order to understand another person, whether or not we like them. I think that it is important to empathize with Vladimir Putin. I have heard an antiterrorism expert say that it is important to empathize with terrorists in order to predict their behavior. Antiterrorism experts do not have a positive attitude toward terrorists. Quite the contrary. Conversely, it is possible, even common, to sympathize with people without empathizing with them. We may not have the opportunity or the inclination to grasp what they are going through in any detail. Perhaps they live on the other side of the world. But we can still feel sympathy for them as fellow humans and wish them well.

or rioting. In emotional contagion, nobody is adopting someone else's emotion in their imagination. The emotion itself spreads from person to person, like yawning sometimes spreads around a room when one person yawns. Also, unlike empathy, emotional contagion does not bring people closer in subjective exchange, and it does not include the usual feature of empathy, which is the attempt by the empathizer to understand the other person and share their experience.

[6] Karsten Stueber (2016, 368) observes that the term "empathy" only started to replace the term "sympathy" at the beginning of the twentieth century. Adam Smith and David Hume use the term "sympathy," yet it seems to me that Hume means something close to empathy in his argument that the foundation of morality is sympathy (*A Treatise of Human Nature*, Part III). Ordinary language is vague on the difference, and I am distinguishing them because they seem to me to be two different feelings arising from different psychological processes. But as I say below, the term itself is less important than my description of a common experience that we can expand to include the imaginative adoption of other states of a person besides their emotions.

Although I have named my model the model of empathy, it does not matter how we define empathy, a contentious topic in the psychological and philosophical literature.[7] I assume that the experience I have described in which I empathize with my friend Pat's grief is a common one, whether or not it has all and only the usual features of human empathy. I am not offering a theory of empathy. I am starting with an experience that I think everyone has had so that we can then imagine expanding that experience to apply to the imaginative adoption of a whole range of psychic states other than emotions and feelings, and we can use that as a model for God's grasp of all a creature's psychic states.

Suppose that you imaginatively project yourself into another person's perspective and attempt to copy other conscious states she has in the same way you attempt to copy her emotion when you empathize with her. We can do that with intimate friends, and we often do that when we are reading a novel. As we imaginatively project ourselves into the character's point of view, we imagine having his or her thoughts, beliefs, feelings, desires, sensations, and emotions, making choices, and acting and experiencing various responses from others, as these states are described by the novelist. Our ability to do all of that is limited by both the novelist's skill and by the fact that we need to depend upon our previous experience to use those descriptions in imagining what it is like to be the character in the narrative. My conjecture is that novelists usually are reasonably successful at conveying visual scenes because they can depend upon the readers' past experiences of seeing virtually all colors and shapes and most elements of nature, which aid readers in imagining something visual. It is harder for the writer to convey sounds and

---

[7] Some writers argue that empathy is "affect matching" in which the empathetic person experiences something close to the feelings of the target person (Snow 2000; De Vignemont and Singer 2006; De Vignemont and Jacob 2012), whereas other researchers argue that a cognitive component of taking on the perspective of the target person is necessary or sufficient for empathy (Goldie 1999; Rameson and Lieberman 2009; Ickes 2003). For a helpful summary of disagreement on the nature of empathy, see John Michael (2014).

smells and tastes. If the writer says the character smells cinnamon, I can bring the fragrance to mind, but if the writer says the character smells tea olive blooms, I do not know what to imagine. The same point applies to tastes and sounds, and it certainly applies to emotions, which is the reason the young have so much trouble understanding narratives in which complex emotions play an important role. Conveying the character's thoughts, beliefs, and decisions is easier because those states are verbally mediated even within the character's own mind, and if the novelist makes the character mentally verbalize, the reader can imagine the character's experience of thinking, believing, and deciding from the character's viewpoint.

There are obviously limitations on our ability to imagine being a character in a novel, but we know how to go about it, and we can easily imagine doing a better job of it. We do what we do when empathizing with someone's feelings. Since we never forget that we are doing this in imagination, there is no problem of confusing who we are with who the character is. We are always aware that the character's beliefs are not our beliefs; the character's sensations are not our sensations; the character's decisions are not our decisions. But we have an imaginative identification with the character that permits us to empathize—very imperfectly, with many different psychic states of the character, and thus to grasp—again very imperfectly—what it is like to be that character.

We can expand this model even farther. What we could call total empathy is empathizing with every one of a person's conscious states throughout that person's entire life—every thought, belief, sensation, mood, desire, and choice, as well as every emotion. What we could call perfect total empathy would be a complete and accurate copy of all a person's conscious states. If A has perfect total empathy with B, then whenever B is in a conscious state C, A acquires a state that is a perfectly accurate copy of C, and A is aware that her conscious state is a copy of C. A is in this way able to grasp what it is like for B to be in state C. Because A is in an empathetic state, A's awareness of her own ego is included in her empathetic state, so an empathetic state always includes something that is not included in the state of the person with whom she is empathizing. B is aware of being B. A is aware of representing B's awareness of being B.

This model needs to be modified for it to be applicable to God as classically understood. In human empathy, the grasp of another person's consciousness is indirect. When I empathize with a friend, I rely upon my own past experience of similar emotions as well as my knowledge of my friend, which I have also acquired from past experience, in forming an imaginative reconstruction of her conscious state. However, on the classical view of God, God's knowledge is direct and nonrepresentational. It is unmediated by concepts, sensory states, memory of past experience, the structure of language, logical inference, or any of the other cognitive aids that we use in the attempt to know the world around us. Some theists will be happy with the idea that God grasps our subjective states by representing them in his imagination, but for those who believe that God's apprehension must be direct, the model needs to be modified.

Can we imagine total perfect empathy that is direct rather than representational? Direct empathy would not be facilitated by anything analogous to a novelist's attempt to convey conscious states of an imaginary character to the reader, nor would it be inferred from behavior, as in our experience of persons in daily life. It would not require a similarity of past experience between God and creatures for God to understand the experience. What we do by relying upon experience God does by directly grasping someone's conscious state. Empathy in God would have to be quite different from empathy in human beings.[8]

---

[8] It can happen that a human person directly perceives another person's feeling and takes it on herself. The empathizer actually has the feeling of the other person. If this happens, the transfer of feeling is direct, but it is not empathy in the sense we want for God if we do not believe that God actually takes on all the feelings of his creatures in response to them. However, some readers might like this variation of the empathy model. I thank Tasia Scrutton for conversation about the possibility of direct empathy.

In empathy, you may be unaware that there is someone empathizing with you. The empathizer's consciousness does not necessarily affect what is going on in your own consciousness, although it can. One of the advantages of the empathy model of omnisubjectivity is that empathy can bring people closer together. Many people have the experience of sharing their consciousness with God as they do with other people, only with God they do not have to worry about clarifying their experience so that he can grasp what it is like. Relationships are always based on a sharing of conscious states that goes both ways. Admittedly, it is pushing the model too far to say that we can empathize with God, but the traditional teaching that grace is a sharing in the divine life is a move in that direction. Aquinas writes, "By the gift of sanctifying grace the rational creature is perfected so that it can freely use not only the created gift itself, but enjoy also the divine person Himself" (*ST* I. q, 43. a. 3. reply obj. 1). Aquinas thought that full union with God is possible only in the enjoyment of the Beatific Vision in heaven, but glimpses of that vision are possible on earth, as many mystics have attested.

The empathy model for omnisubjectivity has some difficulties. As I have described the model, empathy is a state that involves two egos: the ego of the empathizer, and the ego of the target person. The empathizer is always aware of who she is, but when empathizing, she is aware of someone else's awareness. When I empathize with my friend's grief, I am aware of being myself taking on her grief in a part of my consciousness. In the part of my consciousness in which I have empathy—my imagination—I see the world as she sees it, and I take on her feeling. But I also see the world as myself, and I might see or make judgments that differ from her point of view. That is obvious in cases of empathizing with a deluded character in a novel or a movie. I can see the world as the character sees it, but I also see it as delusional when I step back and see it my way.

We are virtually forced to look at empathy this way if we insist that egos really are separate. I see the world as myself; Pat sees as herself;

God sees as himself. But this leads to a problem in empathizing with emotions that fill up a person's consciousness. Suppose that a man is deep in despair. He is aware of nothing but the despair. At least temporarily, it blocks out any other feeling or thought that would permit him to escape it. He cannot assume an outside viewpoint on his situation. To him, his despair is everything. But the empathizer is always aware of something other than the despair because the empathizer is not in despair. The empathizer can have a sense of balance on the life of the person who sees his life as hopeless, but the despairing person cannot. That suggests that the empathizer is not really empathizing completely with the person in despair. As long as there are two egos in the empathizer's consciousness, the empathizer does not accurately grasp despair as it exists in the other person's mind.[9]

Perhaps this objection is not serious enough to ruin the empathy model. Maybe the man in despair does not even want God to fully grasp his despair because he wants help, not total empathy. But whether that is true or not, I think that there is an answer to this objection. Sometimes we can imagine what something would be like if it filled up our consciousness, and we can then confirm it when it happens. Imagine looking at a trompe l'œil painting from the other side of a room. The painting does not take up all your visual field because you also see the frame and other objects in the room. But you can tell what it would look like if it did fill up your visual field. As you move close enough so that it does take up your entire visual space, you see that what it looks like is what you thought it would look like. You were able to imagine what it would be like if the scene filled up your visual field when it did not, and you were able to confirm it when it did.[10] Similarly, God can imagine what it would be like if despair filled up a person's consciousness even though despair never fills up God's consciousness.

---

[9] This objection was given to me by Marilyn Adams shortly before her death.
[10] I thank Tim Mawson for this example and the very helpful conversation about it.

There is another objection to the empathy model that might make the model incoherent. In our experience, empathy is representational, and we might even say that the representational nature of empathy is intrinsic to it. But I have also said that according to the traditional view of God's knowledge, God does not know anything representationally. God knows directly, in a nonmediated way. So, I proposed that omnisubjectivity on this model is direct, nonrepresentational, total empathy. But does that make sense? If empathy is direct, is it still empathy, or is it something else? If we want to emphasize the directness of divine knowing, that suggests the perceptual model.

3.3. The Perceptual Model

Once we say that God knows directly, many people immediately think of perception. We find the idea that God "sees" the world in the Hebrew scriptures, in the writings of many medieval and modern theologians, and among ordinary believers who want an image of divine knowing that is easy to grasp. We need to be reminded that we speak of God seeing only by analogy with human seeing, and like all analogies, there is a point at which it breaks down. The real question is whether it breaks down too soon to be useful, which is the same problem we encounter with the empathy model.

One of the most interesting places in which Aquinas uses the image of God seeing the world is in his attempt to explain how a timeless God can know the past, present, and future in a single grasp. Borrowing from Boethius, Aquinas says that God's knowledge can be compared to a person standing on top of a mountain looking down at a line of people walking on the road below. Each person on the road sees only what is immediately in front of him, but the person on the mountain sees the whole line (*ST* I q. 14 a. 13 reply obj. 3). Of course, Aquinas does not think that God sees as a person on a mountaintop sees. In fact, God does not see at all because he has no visual faculties. But vision is almost always treated as our most important faculty for knowing the world outside of us, and it is natural to use it as a model for divine knowing. If the model can be used for knowing the past and future, can it be used for knowing what is inside creaturely minds?

We can imagine that our minds are transparent to God, and God on the mountaintop sees inside human heads. Perhaps he sees moving images projected as if on a movie screen and hears sounds as if they are coming from a speaker. There is a distance between God the perceiver and you the creature, but that might not be a problem because we also might experience a distance between the self and our seeing and hearing states. When you see, do the sights you have seem like viewing on a screen inside your head? Do not sounds seem like they are coming from the outside? If so, the model might work for visual and auditory images. God could see what we see and hear what we hear by viewing and listening to the same movie in our heads.

The model might also work for perceiving our inner discourse. In Chapter 2 I quoted a line from the Qur'an: "And We have already created man and know what his soul whispers to him, and We are closer to him than [his] jugular vein."[11] God could overhear our speculations, thinking processes, the formation of our beliefs, our deliberations, and what we tell ourselves when we make up our mind to act in a certain way. We do most of this verbally, and so it would be accessible to a being who overhears us in these ways. When we think in pictures, as I do when designing room décor or our landscape, those pictures should also be accessible to a being who can see the same pictures.

But our feelings are different. We *can* observe our feelings, but feeling is not observing. We can tell ourselves our feelings in our inner discourse, but the feeling is not an inner discourse. Pain is

---

[11] Surat Qaf. Qur'an C:50 V.16. https://legacy.quran.com/50/16.

the most obvious example, although not the only one. In Chapter 1 I mentioned the difference between having pain and thinking of one's pain as pain. When we think of our pain as pain, that thought could be overheard by God, but the thought is not the pain. Pain is a conscious state that cannot be seen or heard as in a movie. The perceptual model reaches its limit with the consciousness of feelings. To be conscious of someone's thought that their pain is a pain is not consciousness of the pain; it is consciousness of a thought. Consciousness of pain must be consciousness of the way pain feels. The way pain feels is what it is.

Our desires and many of our feelings have intentional objects, and God's awareness of those states does not imply that God adopts the same intentional object. God's consciousness of my revulsion of snakes is not revulsion of snakes. God's consciousness of someone's desire to harm is not a desire to harm. But revulsion feels a certain way apart from its intentional object, and a desire feels a certain way apart from its object. An omnisubjective God must be aware of the way those states feel, and that awareness cannot be perceptual.

Perhaps the perceptual model can be saved if we use touch rather than vision or hearing as our perceptual analogy for God's grasp of our feelings. Touch is the sense that brings us closer than any other sense to something outside of us. Can you touch someone's pain? We can imagine many more senses than our five, and it is not hard to imagine a sense that brings subject and object even closer than touch. But if the perceptual model is to be helpful, it must be clear that it is not perception from the outside standpoint. That will not work as a model of the grasp of creaturely feelings.

The problem here is the separation of the knower and the known, a separation that Aquinas argued does not apply to God. That problem comes up repeatedly in this book. The problem is not solved by making the knower closer to the known. Provided that there is any distance at all, God as knower does not really grasp what you are experiencing in the way you experience it as the subject of the experience. That seems to push us toward the position

that God literally feels your feeling because you are part of God—
the model of panentheism.

3.4. Panentheism

What if God is omnisubjective because our minds are parts of the
mind of God? Panentheists say that the world is *in* God, but there
are many interpretations of what that means.[12] Philip Clayton
(2017) says that, concisely put, "panentheism is the claim that the
world exists within the Divine, although God is also more than the
world" (2017, 1045). The spatial term "in" is also used by classical
theists, but in a metaphorical sense. Classical theists agree with
panentheists that there is a sense in which the world is in God, and
Aquinas says that explicitly (*ST* I q. 8, a. 1, reply obj. 2). Still, when
we think or feel, we can ask ourselves *who* is thinking or feeling.

In one of the most famous arguments in philosophical history,
Descartes argues in *Meditation II* that the one thing of which he
can be absolutely certain is the existence of his own mind, an argument that each reader can give to themselves. Even if there is an
Evil Genius fooling me about almost everything, I must think in
order to be fooled, so if I believe I am thinking, I can be sure that
I am thinking. But what follows from that? Descartes concludes
convincingly that something must be doing the thinking and that
is what we call "I." He concludes less convincingly that the *I* is a
thinking substance. It is even less certain that I would recognize the
being doing my thinking as myself.

In Descartes' dream hypothesis, he considers the possibility
that he is currently dreaming and asks what that would mean for
the truth of his beliefs. In dreams many beliefs we have about the

---

[12] The issue of how panentheism differs from other forms of theism has been getting
considerable attention in recent philosophy of religion. See, for example, Mullins
(2016a), Gasser (2019), Meister (2017), and Stenmark (2019).

external world are false, although there are a few beliefs that survive doubt even in dreams—most importantly, the existence of oneself, the dreamer. In my dreams my identity is often fluid. I can sometimes be the actor in the events of the dream, and then switch places and be the observer. In a dream I retain memory of my actual past up to a point, but some of my memories are of past dreams. Could I dream that I am a queen in an exotic land, and then wake up to find out that, alas, I am not? Surely that is possible, and it is compatible with Descartes' hypothesis that we could wake up from our entire past life to find out that we are not who we thought we were all these past decades.

In the sixth century BCE, Chuang Tzu briefly describes a dream that is even more radical:

> Once Chuang Chou dreamt he was a butterfly, a butterfly flitting and fluttering around, happy with himself and doing as he pleased. He didn't know he was Chuang Chou. Suddenly he woke up and there he was, solid and unmistakable Chuang Chou. But he didn't know if he was Chuang Chou who had dreamt he was a butterfly, or a butterfly dreaming he was Chuang Chou. Between Chuang Chou and a butterfly there must be *some* distinction. (Chuang Tzu 1964, 45)

Yes, there is some distinction, but there is also something the same in the dreaming and waking states. Chuang Tzu does not mention his memory in his butterfly dream, but it is virtually certain that he could call to mind memories from his past human life in the dream. His dream experience of being a butterfly was the experience of a human imagining he was a butterfly, not the actual experience of a butterfly.

How far is it possible to lose, mistake, or temporarily forget parts of the self and still be the same self? Panentheism stretches those limits and might go beyond them. The most ancient and fascinating version of panentheism or pantheism is the vision of the self in the

Upanishads, which I have already mentioned for its wisdom and lyrical power. These texts say that what we call the self is an illusion. There is only one Self (*Atman*) whose consciousness moves the universe. When I think, feel, dream, it is the Self that is conscious through me. There is no distinction of individual selves within the Self. In Chapter 2 I said that I interpret that to mean that the Self is omnisubjective. But is the price of the omnisubjectivity of a being like *Atman* the nonexistence of *my* conscious self, the one that is different from yours?

That depends. In the Brihadaranyaka Upanishad (IV 8), the great sage Yajnavalkya says that the Self is pure awareness that is surrounded by the senses. At the time of death, the Self leaves the body behind and passes into another state of consciousness. One possibility suggested by the spirituality of the Upanishads is that realizing that my conscious self is really the one Self that moves the universe is like waking up from a dream in which I had assumed an unreal identity. When I wake up, I discover my real self. That self was the dreamer, but I did not realize it in the dream. I did not know that the self that has been conscious of my life all this time is the one Self that is the same for every other self.

As an outsider with little knowledge of Vedic religion or modern Hinduism, I do not know whether it is reasonable to propose that memories of one's past lives are preserved when the sage becomes aware that the consciousness within him is the consciousness of the Self, but one possible interpretation is that the Self includes *all* consciousness—past, present, and future. Suppose that all of one's conscious experiences never disappear; they are contained within the Self. If so, the Self would include my memories as well as the memories of every other conscious self. That could permit the Self to be omnisubjective while still making it possible that we have a form of personal immortality in which we are aware of the difference between our own past life and the lives of others. This interpretation blends Western views of the self with the idea of a single Self that is pure consciousness, and I do not know if that can be done coherently. But I find that non-Western ideas can be helpful for thinking up models that could apply to our own metaphysical positions. Clearly, there are similarities between some varieties of Hinduism and Western panentheism and pantheism.

I mentioned when quoting from the Kena Upanishad in Chapter 2 that there is a difference between saying that the Self is the consciousness that pervades the universe and saying that the Self is a being that has the consciousness that pervades the universe. In the Upanishads, we get the idea that if the human can "wake up" through meditative practices, she would become aware that she is *Atman*, analogous to my waking up to find out that I am not the person in my dream. I am not going to wake up to find out that I am God who has been experiencing my life, but it is possible that I could have a mystical experience in which I become aware that my conscious life is a component of the divine life, as panentheists maintain.

An important historical reason for connecting omnisubjectivity to panentheism is the idea that grasping is union with the object grasped.[13] We find this idea all the way through Western thought from the Pythagoreans to Plato to Plotinus and the neo-Platonic school, and then, through Augustine and the late fifth-century Pseudo-Dionysius, it influenced medieval Christian philosophy and lasted at least until the Renaissance. Like the Pythagoreans, Plotinus combined metaphysics with mystical practice. Plotinus argued that everything that exists emanates from the One, with the material world the last emanation. But in consciousness the human soul can reverse the emanations, and it can merge with the One. Plotinus separates the human being from the One from which it proceeds, but the process of emanation can be reversed in an

---

[13] The following paragraphs on the historical sources of the idea that grasping is uniting are taken from my book, *The Two Greatest Ideas* (2021, ch. 2). I call the idea that the human mind can grasp reality as a whole the first great idea.

experience of sublime unity with the divine. The soul's grasp of the One produces unity with it.

Many Western philosophers have argued that the human being attempts to reach knowledge of God or the One by a process that results in union, but what about God's knowledge of us? Is it a form of uniting with us? The idea that perfect knowledge is union makes it tempting to think so, especially if we accept Aquinas's idea that the subject/object distinction does not apply to God (*ST* I q. 14. a. 2 corpus). The question "Are we a part of God?" probably does not have an easy "yes or no" answer. In a sense we are, and in a sense we are not. Pantheism and panentheism stress "yes," and classical theology stresses "no," but we can find many places in which even the classical tradition permits a version of yes, especially if analogy is permitted.

An example of this point is the versions of panentheism that maintain that everything is in God as the body is in the soul. As I mentioned in the last chapter, Charles Hartshorne (1941) took it to be an ontological truth that the world is God's body, but it can also be taken as an analogy, the position of Richard Swinburne (1977), who refers to Aquinas in support of the analogy. It is interesting that Aquinas accepts the idea that all things are in God, and that creates a problem for his position that God is in all things:

> Further, what is in anything is thereby contained. Now God is not contained by things, but rather does He contain them. Therefore, God is not in things but things are rather in Him. Hence Augustine says (*Octog. Tri. Quaest. Qu.* 20), that *in Him things are, rather than He is in any place.* (*ST* I q. 8, a. 1, obj. 2)

In reply, Aquinas says,

> Although corporeal things are said to be in another as in that which contains them, nevertheless, spiritual things contain those things in which they are; as the soul contains the body. Hence

also God is in things containing them; nevertheless, by a certain similitude to corporeal things, it is said that all things are in God; in as much as they are contained by Him. (reply obj. 2)

So, the soul is in the body, but it contains the body, and similarly, God is in all things, but contains all things. In examining what it means for a spiritual thing to be *in* something, Aquinas seems to come close to panentheism, but of course he is not advocating panentheism. He is recognizing the different senses in which something can be "in" something else. Traditional theists are unwilling to say that we are literally parts of God, but that should not deter them from entertaining the use of spatial locutions borrowed from theories like panentheism.

John W. Cooper's (2006) impressive book on panentheism gives a detailed and sympathetic treatment of the history of panentheism before he offers his objections to it from the perspective of a traditional Christian theist. Those readers attracted to panentheism for reasons independent of the desire to explain how omnisubjectivity is possible will find an enormous number of historical and contemporary versions of panentheism and pantheism described in this book, many of which can be used to explain the possibility of omnisubjectivity. But I want to call attention to Cooper's objections. The objections are partly biblical and partly philosophical. Some are only objections from the position that God is absolutely transcendent and creates the world freely. But one objection that is particularly worrisome is the problem that if the entire created world is in God, that includes evil. Cooper argues that that is incompatible with both God's perfect moral goodness and his holiness. To be fair, this objection has been raised to omnisubjectivity even without a panentheist ontology, and I will address that objection in the next chapter, but panentheism makes the objection especially problematic. Evil is literally in God according to panentheism. That is a serious problem. Perhaps it is an answerable problem, but it is a problem that forces us to confront the classical Greek identities of Being and the Good. What Cooper does not mention is that some philosophers think that it is an advantage of panentheism that the evil of suffering is in God. It should not turn out that God has moral evil in him, but it is a different matter to say that God has suffering in him. Some readers will consider this a problem; some will not.

I have argued that omnisubjectivity is assumed in common practices of prayer. Panentheism has a disadvantage in this respect because it requires us to reconceptualize what is going on when a person prays. In prayer, we often address God in the second person as "you." But if panentheism is an ontological truth, there are no differences among "I," "you," and "he/she/it." At least, there are no differences at the deepest level of reality. I mentioned in Chapter 1 that the first-, second-, and third-person pronouns are called semantic primes because they express conceptual categories that are universal and primitive. It would be disconcerting to find out that when we address God, we are part of the person we address. That is not a proof that panentheism is false, of course, but it is a difficulty that the other models do not have.

All three models I have discussed force us to confront the subject/object distinction, and I believe that that is the heart of the problem of how omnisubjectivity is possible. If God grasps our subjectivity as an object, that is not enough to be an accurate grasp of our subjective states as we experience them. We experience those states as a subject, not as an object. Aquinas rejects the subject/object distinction in his account of God's knowledge, and even in the human case, we encounter puzzles when we attempt to treat other subjects as objects, a central issue in twentieth-century existentialism and phenomenology. The fact that other persons are not objects has important implications for the question of what it means to know another person. Subjectivity is what makes a subject a subject. So, another way to pose the problem for this book is this: How can God know us as subjects?

3.5. Creative Consciousness

To conclude this chapter, I want to approach the question of how God can be omnisubjective from a different direction. I suggest that we reflect on the idea that God is First Cause and conserver of the world. To make these reflections less abstract, I will adopt a metaphor for the relationship between God and the world suggested by a brief remark by Aquinas in which he compares God to light that knows itself. The light metaphor can be combined with anthropomorphic models like the perceptual model or the empathy model. Those models have the advantage of using human knowing faculties as analogues of divine knowing, but both models have the disadvantage of separating God from human subjects, and for that reason, they do not make God's grasp of our first-personal subjective states perfect. For those of us who are not panentheists, we need a way to think of God's knowledge that places the divine consciousness in us without making us part of God. That is the problem I will try to address by investigating the metaphysical implications of this metaphor.

If God knows his own creative power, he must know what he has the power to create in all details, and if God's consciousness keeps everything in existence, God must be continuously aware of everything in the creation in every particular. He does not have to peer outward to find out what's there. What is there is there because God's consciousness keeps it there. God's consciousness extends to everything in existence. It extends to every mode of existence, both subjective and objective. God's consciousness extends to everything there is.

If everything is within God's consciousness, it does not follow that everything is within God, so this observation does not entail panentheism. Even in humans, our consciousness extends far beyond the limits of ourselves as human organisms. Our consciousness keeps expanding with experience and reflective thought, and we can sometimes feel that there is a sense in which the self expands along with our consciousness. But when I grasp events in other parts of the world or other parts of the cosmos, I do not think that those events are part of me. Perhaps that is because I situate myself in space, but, of course, the spatial terms "out" and "in" are misleading as applied to God. I assume that God has no shape or boundary, and he is not situated in a certain place relative to everything else that exists. That is one of the reasons that the difference between panentheism and classical theism is vague.

In the course of discussing the idea that God knows everything in existence through his knowledge of himself, Aquinas says that if light knew itself, it would know all colors (ST I q. 14 a. 6 corpus). All colors preexist in white light. This simple remark makes me visualize all creation coming out of God like light streaming from its source in the divine consciousness to produce a colorful universe. We could compare each subjective state to a distinct color in an infinite rainbow of colors flowing out of the divine light. Since each colored ray exists within God's consciousness, God knows all subjectivity in the universe perfectly through his consciousness of himself as the source of light. All subjective experience, like every other aspect of the created world, exists because it comes out of God with God's continual awareness attached to it.

An advantage of the light metaphor is that light bathes and infuses objects without being identical with them. Not all actual physical objects are transparent, of course, but we can imagine light powerful enough to create and infuse everything it creates. If light of that kind knew itself, as Aquinas imagines, its consciousness of itself would include consciousness of everything it penetrates. We can also imagine that every created thing is sustained by the photons streaming through it. If the stream of photons ceased, the object would go from the light of existence to the darkness of nonexistence. Some divine light creates further light, or creaturely consciousness, and some of that is creative. The power of creaturely creativity flows from the divine creative power.

I like the light metaphor because it helps us to see the possibility that God is in us and through us without being us. If God is in our sensations and feelings, he knows what they feel like. God must have known what he was doing when he created sensations like pain and pleasure and emotions like love and hate. As creator, he knows what he created. If so, he must be able to grasp what those states feel like since, to repeat, the way they feel is what they are. To know pain is to know the way pain feels. To know love is to know the way love feels. To know fear is to know the way fear feels. The divine consciousness is a unity like white light, but contained within that unity is every conscious experience any being has like white light contains an infinite rainbow of colors.

Aquinas writes, "Now God could not be said to know Himself perfectly unless He knew all the ways in which His own perfection can be shared by others. Neither could He know the very nature of being perfectly unless He knew all modes of being. Hence it is manifest that God knows all things with proper knowledge, in their distinction from each other" (*ST* I q. 14 a. 6 end of corpus). I conclude that pain and pleasure, love and hate, sorrow and joy, and every human cognitive and affective state preexist in the divine consciousness as blue and yellow preexist in white light. But God is conscious of each color simultaneously, and by analogy, God is conscious of pain simultaneously with his consciousness of pleasure, joy, love, fear, hate, and all the other experiences we have. God grasps every good conscious state and every bad conscious state in one eternal moment. Does God actually feel pain? That depends upon whether the perfect grasp of a feeling is a feeling. Let's look at this more carefully.

Here is an argument that the imaginative grasp of someone's feeling is a feeling. The way a feeling feels is what it is, so to grasp what it is to grasp the way it feels. To grasp the way it feels is to feel it. To grasp the way it feels perfectly is to feel it exactly the way the other person feels it. Perfect empathy with a feeling is a feeling.

If God has perfect empathy, God feels all the feelings of all his creatures.

This approach arises from the view that the imagination in human beings is an imperfect way to grasp reality. We have inherited the empiricist position that our imagination is like sensory states or emotional states, differing from those states in being fainter and deficient, as Hume proposes at the beginning of the *Treatise*. In God there is no imperfection, so it seems to follow that perfectly grasping your sensation of red is seeing red; perfectly grasping your feeling of pain is feeling pain; perfectly grasping your hunger is feeling hungry—and so on.

Another reason this argument is tempting is that our imaginings give us feelings all the time. We have feelings when we are reading a novel or watching a film and the character is in a frightening or exciting situation. That makes us feel frightened or excited, and research on mirror neurons has led to the conjecture that the same neurons fire in our brain when we see or think about somebody who is frightened as when we are frightened ourselves.[14] When we empathize with someone, we often feel the same kind of feeling that they feel. That can obviously happen, and so we might conclude that grasping a feeling in the imagination is a feeling.

Some readers might be content with this conclusion, but I think that the argument goes wrong at the premise: "To grasp the way it feels is to feel it." When humans imagine a feeling, we usually rely upon our memory of past experiences in which we felt something similar. Our imaginations recreate experience, and we think that the better the imagination, the closer it is to an actual experience.

---

[14] A mirror neuron is one that fires both when an animal acts and when the animal observes the same action done by another animal. Although mirror neurons have not been observed in humans, it has led to speculation that the neurological accompaniment to the awareness of another person's intentions or feelings is the same as the neurological accompaniment to the awareness of the same intentions or feelings in oneself. See Iacobini et al. (2005).

So, it is tempting to say that (1) imagination copies a previous experience, and (2) perfect imagination of an experience is an experience.

The empiricist principle that experience must precede imagination is probably false even for humans, but in any case, it has to be false for God. God does not have to see red before he can imagine it. It is because God imagines red that anyone is able to see red. It would be very implausible and limiting on God to say that he needs to experience something before he can imagine it. So, assumption (1) is false for God. God does not have to first experience seeing red in order to imagine seeing red. God does not have to first experience pain before he can imagine feeling pain.

But that does not yet tell us that there is a difference between feeling fear and grasping what fear feels like in the imagination, or feeling pain and grasping what pain feels like in the imagination. But think of horror movies. Many people enjoy imaginative fear, but they would hate real fear, so there must be a difference. Some people imagine future pain and hope that imagining it will prepare them for it when it happens. Suppose that it has been a long time since you had an injection, so your memory of it is vague. But you are about to get a shot, and you imagine what it will be like. (Not a good idea, but you do it anyway.) When you get the shot and feel the pain, you might say to yourself, "Oh, yes, what I was imagining is what it feels like." You knew what the pain feels like when you were not feeling pain, and when you did feel it, you confirmed to yourself that what you had been imagining was correct. But can you also grasp what something feels like that you have never felt? Even that might be possible. Perhaps it can happen when someone reads about mystical experiences that they have never had. They imagine what it would be like to have St. Teresa's experience. Isn't it possible that eventually they do have the experience, and that they then say to themselves, "Yes, that is what I thought it would be like." But they do not say, "When I was imagining the experience, I had it." They knew in imagination what it would be like, but knowing that is not the same as having the experience.[15]

I cannot verify my suggestion that a human being can grasp what an experience is like when she never had the experience, but when it comes to God, there is no reason at all to think that God cannot imagine what an experience is like without experiencing it previously, nor do we need to conclude that perfectly grasping what an experience is like in imagination is the same as having it. I suggest, then, that both (1) and (2) above are false for God.[16]

When I think about God's creative consciousness, I imagine the created universe flowing out of the divine being, so God is transcendent. But God is immanent in every part of the created universe since it exists and continues to exist because the divine consciousness continuously grasps it like light that continuously infuses every actual being. I am using light as a metaphor, as Aquinas did in the line I quoted above, but it is interesting that in *Genesis*, light is the first product of creation, the part of creation closest to the divine being. "Then God said, 'Let there be light,' and there was light." (Gen. 1:3, NRSV). Light is the most ethereal component of the material world, and it has been a focus of religious art and theological reflection for many centuries.

An enthralling reference to God as light appears in St. Augustine's description of an experience he had in meditation:

> Being admonished by all this to return to myself, I entered into my own depths, with You as guide; and I was able to do it because You were my helper. I entered, and with the eye of my soul, such as it was, I saw Your unchangeable Light shining over that same eye of my soul, over my mind. It was not the light of everyday that the eye of flesh can see, nor some greater light of the same order,

---

[15] I am grateful to Tim Mawson for giving me the idea in this paragraph.

[16] In Zagzebski (2008) I claimed that a perfect empathetic copy of a feeling is a feeling. Since then I have changed my mind.

such as might be if the brightness of our daily light should be seen shining with a more intense brightness and filling all things with its greatness. Your Light was not that, but other, altogether other, than all such lights. (*Confessions* 7:10)

St. Bonaventure was fascinated with light, arguing that the light referred to at the beginning of *Genesis* is not spiritual light, as Augustine argued, but corporeal light (Houser and Noone 2013, Bk II, distinction 13, art 1, q. 1). He proceeded to investigate light at length, arguing that light is purely active, but it is not a substance since if it were, it would be God. Light makes matter visible, and the hierarchy of bodies corresponds to the hierarchy of things capable of partaking either more or less in the light that renders bodies active and extended (Houser and Noone 2013, Bk II, d. 13, art. 2).[17]

Aquinas refers to the supernatural power of light in his stunning description of the way he imagines the end of the world in which all the elements of the world will be glorified by light, the stars of the sky becoming brighter, the resurrected human body clear as crystal (*ST* Sup to Third part, q. 85 a. 1, corpus), and the renewed earth translucent and glowing with light: "[I]t is said that the earth on its outward surface will be as transparent as glass, water as crystal, the air as heaven, fire as the lights of heaven" (*ST* Sup to Third part, q. 91, a. 4 corpus). That suggests to me that Aquinas thought that the surface of the earth will look like stained glass. The light of God glorifies the creation.

Light is fascinating. No matter how much we know about the physics of light and its property of making bodies luminous, I think that light is the closest physical analogue of the divine consciousness within us. It no doubt appeals to the mind of the artist more than to the metaphysician, but it is a riveting image of God's ability

---

[17] See also commentary in the *Stanford Encyclopedia of Philosophy* entry on St. Bonaventure by Noone and Houser.

to grasp our conscious states without violating our identity as individual selves.

In this chapter I have presented four approaches to the possibility of omnisubjectivity. I know that different readers will have different preferences based on their previous theological positions, so it is useful to look at more than one. Another advantage of multiple models is that we see that their advantages and disadvantages differ, so moving from one to another can give us a sense of proportion on our limited cognitive abilities, and the conviction that God's relationship to the created world transcends them all.[18]

---

[18] I thank Tasia Scrutton for suggesting this advantage of multiple models.

4

Objections from Other Attributes

4.1. Introduction

People often tell me that they find omnisubjectivity plausible, whether they are classical theists or theists who are comfortable with modifying some of the traditional attributes. I have defended omnisubjectivity partly by arguing that it is entailed by the attributes of omniscience and omnipresence, but there are other classical attributes that appear to conflict with omnisubjectivity—for instance, timelessness, immutability, and impassibility. Although there have been many objections to these attributes in recent history, they are part of a long tradition. Notice that if omniscience and omnipresence entail omnisubjectivity, but omnisubjectivity is inconsistent with one or more of these other attributes, then the classical set of divine attributes is inconsistent.

Moral perfection and holiness are also attributes that apparently conflict with omnisubjectivity. Moral perfection seems to make it impossible for God to fully grasp what it is like to hate, or to feel wrathful, or resentful, or vengeful. I have also heard the worry that it is incompatible with divine holiness to fully grasp feelings that are not morally wrong, but are inappropriate for a divine being, such as sexual feelings. Another problem is that the infinite nature of God seems to make it impossible for God to fully grasp from a creature's perspective what it is like to be in states that are essentially connected with finitude—states like bewilderment, confusion, or fear. If accurately grasping such states necessarily requires experiencing states that are incompatible with the nature of an infinite deity, God cannot fully grasp those states.

Omnisubjectivity. Linda Trinkaus Zagzebski, Oxford University Press. © Oxford University Press 2023.
DOI: 10.1093/oso/9780197682098.003.0004

The tension between omnisubjectivity and these attributes is important, both for philosophers who welcome the way omnisubjectivity reinforces their belief that the classical view of God needs to be revised, and even more so for those philosophers who are committed to the classical conception but hope to integrate omnisubjectivity into that conception.

It is significant that apart from omnisubjectivity, the traditional conception of God includes many attributes that apparently conflict with each other, and the attempt to resolve these conflicts has kept philosophical theologians busy for centuries, with a burst of analytical work in the last fifty years. To mention a few, perfect goodness entails the inability to sin, but that seems to conflict with omnipotence and with divine freedom.[1] Since a timeless being cannot know what time it is, timelessness seems to conflict with omniscience.[2] The attribute of impassibility seems incompatible with the ability of God to lovingly interact and respond emotionally to his creatures, and that is one of the reasons for the popularity of the position that God suffers.[3] There is also the problem of the connection between God's will and necessary truths since necessity seems to constrain God's will and prevent him from being omnipotent.[4] There are other apparent conflicts, and traditionalists have been engaged in a laudable attempt to defend the coherence of all the attributes of God defended by the church fathers, and Anselm, Aquinas, and their many successors. This work is energized by the conviction that the supremely perfect being must have all these properties, and therefore, there must be a way to explain their coherence. I am

[1] See Pike (1969), Carter (1982), and Morris (1983) for the problem that God's inability to sin appears to be incompatible with omnipotence. See also discussion by Wierenga (1989, ch. 7).

[2] One of the earliest papers arguing for a conflict between timelessness and omniscience is Prior (1962). See also Norman Kretzmann (1966), Nelson Pike (2002), Nicholas Wolterstorff (1982), and discussion by Edward Wierenga (1989, ch. 6).

[3] It is common to believe that God suffers with us, but see Weinandy (2000) for a defense of God's impassibility against the position that a suffering God is more loving.

[4] See Leftow (2012) for an extensive treatment of the relationship between God and necessary truths.

proposing that omnisubjectivity should be added to the traditional list, so it is not surprising that it apparently conflicts with some of the other properties in our conception of the supreme being. In some cases, the argument that divine omnisubjectivity is consistent with other attributes can borrow from arguments that the other attributes are consistent with each other. In other cases, a new argument is needed. In every case, each person will want to evaluate how important it is to defend a specific account of an attribute with which they begin reflection, and whether it is acceptable or even desirable to modify that conception after reflection.

4.2. Timelessness and Immutability

Let us start with the problem that omnisubjectivity appears to be incompatible with immutability and timelessness. Timelessness and immutability go together on classical views of time deriving from Aristotle, who defined time as the measure of change (*Physics* IV, ch. 11). A temporal being is changeable; a timeless being is unchangeable. It is not obvious that any temporal being must be changeable, but I think it is fair to say that most philosophical theologians put temporality and mutability together and timelessness and immutability together. In any case, the issue of whether a temporal being can be immutable will not affect my arguments.

Many philosophers and theologians are willing to deny timelessness and immutability for reasons that have nothing to do with my proposal in this book, but it would be an advantage if omnisubjectivity is compatible with these attributes because that would mean that the property of omnisubjectivity does not force us to deny two properties that have long been closely associated with the transcendence of God. Philosophers who stress divine immanence and argue that the attributes of timelessness and immutability must be rejected often find omnisubjectivity appealing (e.g., Mullins 2022), but classical theists who are committed to these attributes have also sometimes endorsed omnisubjectivity (e.g., Blankenhorn 2016). It would be an advantage if omnisubjectivity is defensible either way.

I assume that God grasps the sequence of temporal events. At a minimum, God is present at each moment of time in the same way Aquinas and Anselm say that God is present at each point of space. I have already argued that being present at each point in space does not require being a spatial being. Likewise, being present at each moment of time does not require being a temporal being. I assume also that God has direct, intimate knowledge of everything going on at each moment of time. What omnisubjectivity adds is perfect knowledge of each conscious experience from the first-person viewpoint of the subject. Does that raise any greater problem for a timeless and immutable God than the general problem of intimate acquaintance with all temporal and spatial events?

I think not, but let's look more closely at the grasp of temporality. An omnisubjective being must know what it is like to experience time. He knows what it is like to anticipate an event, to hope for it to happen, to be excited when it happens, and sad when it is over. He knows what it is like to dread an event and to be relieved when it is past. He must also know what it is like to go through a temporally extended process, whether it is a short process like brushing your teeth, or a long process like writing a book. It is an essential part of all these states that they involve temporal duration and change. But defenders of divine temporality sometimes say that a being cannot know what it is like to experience temporal duration and change without experiencing temporal duration and change.[5] And if experiencing temporal duration and change requires temporality, then God's experience of temporal duration and change would entail that he is temporal.

---

[5] See R. T. Mullins (2016b) for recent arguments that a timeless God cannot experience temporal duration and change.

This problem exists whether or not God is omnisubjective, although omnisubjectivity highlights the issue. I agree that an omnisubjective being knows what it is like to experience temporal duration, and he must have direct acquaintance with the experience of temporal sequence, but does it necessarily follow that he must exist in time? There are models of the way a timeless being could grasp temporal duration in the literature that would also apply to a timeless and omnisubjective being.[6] Models like these might succeed and they might not. If they succeed, they can be used by a defender of an omnisubjective timeless deity. If they do not, timelessness fails apart from omnisubjectivity. Omnisubjectivity is not the culprit. Is a timeless being's grasp of a subjective sequence any harder than a timeless being's grasp of a temporal sequence in nature? Even aside from omnisubjectivity, the defender of timelessness needs an account of how a timeless being can grasp the temporal sequence of a star burning through the elements in its core, then collapsing and violently exploding, creating a neutron star. Is that any different than the problem of how a timeless being can grasp the temporal sequence of anticipation, waiting, boredom, and relief? Whether God grasps an objective sequence in nature or a subjective sequence in nature, the problem is the grasp of temporal sequence by a timeless being.

But this might not yet be a satisfactory answer. It is reasonable to think of the difference between timelessness and temporality as a difference in point of view on the same thing. The same thing grasped from a temporal point of view can be grasped from a timeless point of view. The point of view does not alter what is grasped.

---

[6] Eleonore Stump and Norman Kretzmann (1981) develop the concept of atemporal duration to explain how a timeless God can grasp events in time. In his book on eternity, Brian Leftow (1991) denies that if a being X knows a changing thing as changing, then X undergoes change, and he offers two models to support his view (342–348). Although Leftow does not discuss a property like omnisubjectivity, his second model is one in which God is aware of our awareness, and he says it would apply to knowing colors and what it is like to be a bat. More recently, Katherin Rogers (2020) defends the compatibility of all the traditional divine attributes, including timeless eternity and omniscience.

So, a timeless deity can grasp a sequence of events in objective nature like the explosion of a star because the point of view of the timeless viewer is independent of the events and does not alter them. But the perspective of a conscious subject going through a temporal experience is what the experience is. To grasp that experience from a timeless perspective is to change it into something else. A timeless God cannot get what it is like to wait, and wait, and wait, getting more bored with each passing second. To grasp what it is like to experience the passage of time as boring, one must experience the passage of time. To experience the passage of time, God must be in time, or so it can be argued.

The adherent of timeless omnisubjectivity can turn to the empathy model to answer this objection. In the empathy model, when God empathizes with your grief, God does not grieve. God can empathize with your experience of smelling roses without smelling roses. God can empathize with your boredom without being bored. If the empathy model works for smelling roses, it should work for feeling bored.

Think again about the way we empathize with the experience of a character in a novel. Rarely do we imagine the character's experience in real time. Usually, our conscious representation of the character's experience is temporally compressed. We experience in a few seconds a copy of what the character goes through in several minutes or hours. Sometimes it can be the reverse. Our empathetic experience can take longer than the experience of the character, as when the novelist intentionally stretches out the description of an event that would take only a few seconds (Henry James does that). My point is that the empathetic copy of an experience need not have the same temporal duration as the experience it copies, and in fact, typically does not. I also think that a temporally compressed copy of an experience need not be inferior because of the temporal compression. Of course, human empathy is defective, but I do not see any reason to think that it is defective because of temporal compression. If I am right about that, we can imagine a being whose empathy with someone's experience is compressed to a single eternal instant. God grasps in a flash what it feels like to go through a temporally extended experience of boredom, or of eager anticipation, waiting, and joy—or of dread, followed by pain, and then relief.

What about the other models of omnisubjectivity? The panentheist who says that God is in time and can experience time does not have the problem addressed here. I think that the perceptual model, like the empathy model, has no special problem in explaining God's timeless perception of temporally extended feelings and other psychic states. If the model works for perceiving a sequence of events in nature, it should work for perceiving subjective states with temporal duration. Earlier I mentioned the analogy Aquinas uses in describing how a timeless being can perceive events in time. He says that perceiving temporal events from an atemporal standpoint is like standing on the top of a mountain observing the travelers on a road below. The travelers do not see behind them, and they see only what is immediately in front of them, but the observer on the mountain sees the whole line of travelers walking along the road. This model has deficiencies because the viewer is in time and can see the travelers moving, but I do not think that there is any additional problem in seeing into their temporal states of consciousness. If a timeless God can see their legs moving, he can see their frustration and boredom. Again, I do not deny that there are deep problems in understanding how a timeless God grasps a temporal creation, and I am not defending timelessness, but I do not see that adding omnisubjectivity to timelessness creates any problems that are not already there.

I like the idea that subjective states flow out of God with his continuous awareness of them attached. As new subjective states emerge in the consciousness of a creature, God's awareness continues. That idea helps to show how God can experience us as subjects, not objects, while respecting the difference between God and ourselves. My arguments in Chapter 3 led to the conclusion that God must know what a feeling feels like in his imagination since the way it feels is what it is. So, God must have an imaginative feeling of boredom when he grasps what our boredom is. Can that feeling be grasped in an eternal flash outside of time? I don't know why not, but I do not insist upon it.

4.3. Impassibility

The attribute of impassibility has a long history in the Christian tradition. To define it in the most general way, it is the property of being unmoved by anything outside of God. If God is immutable, God cannot be changed by anything, whether internal or external, so if being moved means being changed, an immutable God is impassible. But impassibility is currently a disputed topic because it was traditionally interpreted as entailing that God does not feel emotions. That is for two reasons. First, many emotions were called passions (*passiones*) or forms of being moved by something else, but God is not moved by anything outside the divine nature. Second, according to Aristotle, *passiones* reside in the sensitive appetite and require a body, but God has no body.[7] The idea that God shares in our emotions is probably now the dominant position. Does omnisubjectivity entail that God is passible? If so, is that a problem?

Traditional Islam has a similar problem about divine emotions because Muslims also inherited the position of Aristotle that emotions require a body and involve changes in consciousness caused by something external. Since Allah does not change his consciousness, Allah does not have emotions, and of course, Allah does not have a body. But like the Hebrew and Christian scriptures, the Qur'an refers to Allah's great mercy and love, and sometimes

---

[7] See Scrutton (2011, ch. 1) for a very helpful summary of the ideas of passibility and impassibility in the early Church and in modern theology.

anger and joy. I interpret Islam as facing the same difficulty as classical Christian theology in reconciling divine impassibility with the desire to think of God as a personal agent who desires intimate relationships with his creatures.

Suppose that God or Allah feels emotions in response to his creatures. Does that mean his consciousness is changed by something external? Not necessarily. It depends upon whether being "moved" by the world requires change. God could be immutably "moved" by the world he created by changelessly knowing what is going on in the world and even changelessly responding to human emotions. I see no reason why God could not timelessly and unchangingly grasp our subjective states, including knowing what our suffering feels like in his imagination. And he can eternally and unchangingly respond to those states.

Let's take a closer look at the Aristotelian positions about emotions adopted by Aquinas. One is that passions (*passiones*) are in the sensitive appetite and require a body. The other is that emotions are called *passiones* because they are passive, but that is contrary to the divine nature since God is Pure Act. These arguments would be a problem for omnisubjectivity if they demonstrate that God is impassible and omnisubjectivity entails that God is passible. But does it?

It is worth noticing first that not all the states we now call emotions are in the category of *passiones*. Examples of *passiones* given by Aquinas include love, hate, fear, anger, pleasure, sorrow, hope, and despair. To have these emotions, God would have to be the passive recipient of a state caused by an external being like a human creature, so God does not have these emotions (*Summa Contra Gentiles* I, sec. 89, cited as SCG in what follows). In contrast, Aquinas designates some of the states we classify as emotions as *affectiones*.[8] These states are in the rational appetite. They include

[8] Norman Kretzmann's translation of "*affectiones*" is "attitudes" (1997, ch. 8). Kretzmann chooses a word that makes it clear that *affectiones* do not have an aspect of feeling.

joy and a higher kind of love (SCG I sec. 90–91). They are not passive and do not require a body. God has *affectiones* but not *passiones*.

The distinction between *affectiones* and *passiones* may show that Aquinas's position on divine emotions is not as radical as it first appears, but the distinction is of no use to the defender of omnisubjectivity because an omnisubjective God grasps what it is like to feel *passiones* as well as *affectiones*. Aquinas' objection to the divine grasp of *passiones* is that grasping *passiones* requires a body and makes God passive.

In the first place, I see no reason to think that an emotion like fear necessarily requires a body. If it requires a body in humans, that cannot be because of any necessary connection between emotional states and bodies. It would only be because of the way the human mind connects with the human body. Descartes' thought experiment of imagining any psychic state you wish without a body is enough to convince most philosophers that a body is not metaphysically necessary for any conscious state, including *passiones* like fear, pain and pleasure, and love and hate.

Second, the position that *passiones* are passive is surely too extreme. These emotions are produced from the combination of a capacity in the being feeling the emotion and a stimulus for the emotion, which can be either internal or external. But something external is in part the cause of many emotions and psychic states like empathy. God cannot empathize unless there is something there with which to empathize. But there is something there because God wills it to be there. God could changelessly will to grasp human emotions and to empathize with those emotions. If so, God's grasp of what those emotions are like is willed by himself. God is not passively inflicted with empathy. God can unchangingly grasp human emotions by unchangingly willing to do so. And if I was right in the last chapter, God's empathetic grasp is not an emotional state. It is not a state of passion, so even if God is impassible, the divine empathetic grasp of our passions is not a passion.

Some readers might prefer the perceptual model. When God perceives your pain, using whatever divine faculty is appropriate, God is affected by you and so is not wholly independent of you, even if God is able to perceive your pain without changing. But is this problem any different than the problem that whatever God perceives, whether it is an objective event like the snow falling on the mountains, or a subjective state like your feeling of sadness, he is affected by something outside of him? I doubt it. Aquinas attempted to solve this problem by arguing that God knows everything in existence through his own essence, and so he is not affected by anything going on outside of him. If that account works for divine knowledge of objective events, it should work for divine knowledge of subjective states like emotions. If the account does not work, it is no greater of a problem for omnisubjectivity than for knowledge of contingent objective events. This is another example of how omnisubjectivity calls attention to problems about God's knowledge of the created world that are there anyway.

God ultimately causes and is continuously aware of all subjective states as well as all objective events. God grasps all subjective states simultaneously through his own consciousness. Is God impassible? In a sense yes, and in a sense no. God knows what your suffering is like in his imagination, and God would not do that unless you are suffering. So, God is affected by you and in that sense is passible. But on the other hand, your suffering is itself ultimately caused by and sustained in existence by God's own consciousness, and he wills it to be so. That does not look like passibility in the sense of passivity.

If God has emotions in response to us, God would be passible for reasons independent of omnisubjectivity. I will not address those reasons here because they are not a part of the attribute of omnisubjectivity. I conclude that omnisubjectivity does not make God passive, and omnisubjectivity certainly does not require a body; omnisubjectivity does not have the consequence that God feels emotions. So, omnisubjectivity is compatible with impassibility. I agree that God might be passible for other reasons, but not because of omnisubjectivity.[9]

Ryan Mullins (2022) proposes that there are difficulties in combining omnisubjectivity and passibility with timelessness and immutability. He argues that if God suffers and is timeless, God suffers timelessly. His concern is that God would be locked into a timeless present of eternal torment that will never cease.

It seems to me that this argument falters in more than one place. First, it depends upon which model of omnisubjectivity we are using and whether the imaginative grasp of suffering is suffering. I have said that perceiving suffering is not suffering. Empathizing with suffering is imaginative suffering, which is not suffering. But let's suppose for the sake of argument that divine consciousness of suffering as it is experienced by the subject *is* suffering. Some readers will probably take that position. Mullins interprets that to mean that a timeless God would suffer torment that never begins and never ends and has no succession. What is the problem here? The image of timeless suffering needs to be put into a perspective in which everything God experiences is timeless and simultaneous, including timeless joy, happiness, and love. I appreciate the worry that the eternal grasp of torment might spoil the eternal grasp of bliss, but it does not help to say that God is temporal and passible, as Mullins maintains. A temporal and passible God would experience suffering, and surely it is unlikely that a temporal God forgets the suffering. In fact, on the temporality view, God's suffering would last for a long time and would never be forgotten. That seems worse than divine suffering that exists in one nontemporal instant.

Mullins has another argument. If we accept both simplicity and omnisubjectivity, and if an omnisubjective God suffers, then it seems to follow that suffering is the divine essence.[10] I proposed in

---

[9] Brian Leftow (2012, 285–286) argues that God could feel emotions even though he is timeless and immutable. He does not directly speak of passibility there, but his position permits the possibility that God is timelessly and immutably feeling with us.

[10] Mullins says he got the idea for this objection from Blankenhorn (2016, 458). Blankenhorn does not conclude that suffering is the divine essence, but Mullins argues

Chapter 3 that the divine essence is the divine consciousness, which includes the grasp of all creaturely conscious states, including creaturely suffering. But if the imaginative grasp of suffering is not suffering, the conclusion does not follow. Again, there will be readers who take the position that the imaginative grasp of suffering is suffering. Let's make that assumption and assume also that we accept the doctrine of simplicity according to which all of God's states/properties/acts are identical with the divine essence. There is no distinction between one state and another, between one act and another, between one attribute and another. All of it is God's essence. So, God telling Moses to go to Pharaoh is the divine essence; God's love for all his children is the divine essence; God's power and goodness and infinity are the divine essence. Everything we can say about God is the divine essence according to the doctrine of simplicity. It follows that if God actually feels your pain, that feeling of pain is identical with the divine essence. Is this a problem? It could be problematic for the same reason that it is problematic to say that God talking to Moses is identical with the divine essence. I will not deny that those who accept both the doctrine of simplicity and the position that God feels our feelings need an answer to this objection, but I think that they can point out that some of God's states, such as talking to Moses and feeling pain, would be states that he chose to have, whereas others, like necessary being and pure goodness, would not be.[11] This difference is compatible with the basic metaphysical idea that God is one act of pure being. In any case, I have argued that omnisubjectivity does not commit us to the position that God feels our feelings, and it is neutral on the doctrine of simplicity. I will leave it to others to work out whether the set of

that that is a consequence of combining omnisubjectivity with timelessness and simplicity. Blankenhorn is a classical theist who endorses omnisubjectivity.

[11] The problem here lies in the apparent conflict between divine simplicity and God's free choice. Stump and Kretzmann (1985) addressed this problem several decades ago in a paper defending Aquinas's interpretation of absolute simplicity. Their defense lies in an interpretation of God's will that rejects the modern idea that the will is a neutral faculty for choosing among alternatives. God's will is both free and conditionally necessitated.

traditional divine attributes including simplicity and impassibility is so logically tight that removing one of them leads to the crash of the whole house of cards. My purpose in this book is to add a card to the stack.

Mullins concludes that I and other defenders of omnisubjectivity should give up the classical attributes of timelessness, immutability, impassibility, and simplicity, and join theists like himself who adopt a conception in which God is temporal and changeable, permitting himself to be moved by his creatures and sharing in lives of suffering for a redemptive purpose. Omnisubjectivity is an attribute in which God shares in our lives by perfectly grasping everything we go through. I agree with Mullins about that. God might also emotionally respond to us, in which case God would be passible, but that is not part of omnisubjectivity. I conclude that omnisubjectivity is compatible with the classical attributes. There are objections to those attributes for reasons that are independent of omnisubjectivity, but omnisubjectivity is not the problem.

I think that omnisubjectivity is very important for both theology and religious practice. It generates puzzles, but I am hoping that it will be accepted by philosophers and theologians whose previous theological perspectives vary greatly. Each perspective has its own difficulties. It is interesting that by far the greatest attention in discussions of omnisubjectivity is on the divine grasp of emotion and feeling. Feeling states are by no means the only first-person conscious states, but feelings highlight the problem of grasping something that requires absorbing it into the mind of the omnisubjective knower. Grasping someone's intention to commit a crime from their first-person viewpoint is not as threatening to the classical conception of God as grasping someone's hateful feeling from their first-person perspective, but the problem is just one of degree. Charles Hartshorne (1934) argued that every human conscious state has some affective tone, presumably even the thought that $2 + 2 = 4$. Some states are accompanied only by a faint feeling; others are much more intense. For some, the feeling is the entire state. This is a very strong position, and I am not endorsing it, but I think that we can say at a minimum that an enormous number of subjective states of both humans and animals are feelings, and many other conscious states are accompanied by feelings. A perfect grasp of a feeling state or a state that is partly a feeling requires grasping how the feeling feels. I have also argued that grasping how a feeling feels is not feeling it. God grasps the feelings of creatures in his imagination. That is a perfection.

Integrating omnisubjectivity into one's previous theological theories is a challenge, but it is no challenge at all to integrate it into one's previous forms of religious practice. The theoretical challenge differs for theists of different kinds, and although I adhere as closely as I can to the classical view we have inherited, I believe that omnisubjectivity can be combined with a variety of approaches to timelessness, immutability, and impassibility. Those philosophers who believe that God has emotions have already given up impassibility, and do not worry if omnisubjectivity entails passibility. But I have argued that whether omnisubjectivity entails that God has our emotions rests on positions on the divine imagination and the nature of divine empathy. The more God's imagination looks like ours, the more likely it seems that God feels our emotions. But my brief journey into the idea of creative consciousness in the last chapter was intended to show that like light, which permeates a transparent object, God permeates our feelings without taking on the feeling itself. If that is possible, it is possible that God fully grasps our feelings while maintaining his impassibility. If God is passible, it is not because of omnisubjectivity.

4.4. The Moral Objection and the Holiness Objection

Omnisubjectivity would be a problem if some conscious states are immoral, and even the perfect grasp of such states is immoral.

Clearly, there are immoral conscious states. If an act is morally wrong, the conscious decision to perform the act is wrong. Motivational states and certain emotions are probably wrong as well—for example, hate, envy, and spite. There are probably also morally wrong beliefs, such as the belief that some person deserves to be tortured. There are so many examples, it does not matter if I am mistaken about some of them. Undoubtedly, there are morally wrong conscious states, at least among humans.

But if a state is wrong, is it wrong to accurately grasp it in one's own mind? That depends upon what makes the state immoral and the model of grasping we are using. The perceptual model of omnisubjectivity can avoid the conclusion that God feels his creature's hate or sadistic pleasure because that model maintains a distance, however small, between God the perceiver and the creaturely feeling. That is both an advantage and a disadvantage of the model. The advantage is that the moral objection does not arise. The disadvantage is that the model prevents God from fully grasping the subject as a subject. I realize that some readers will prefer this model, but I think that getting it to work as a way to avoid the moral objection is like sailing between Scylla and Charybdis. The closer God is to the subject, the more it seems that the subject's feeling touches God. But any distance between God and the subject seems to prevent God from accurately grasping the subject's state from the subject's viewpoint.

The empathy model is a more promising model for grasping a subject as a subject, but for that reason, the moral objection is more threatening. It depends upon what happens in an empathetic state. If a character in a novel is vicious, is there anything wrong with empathizing with that character's vicious feelings, beliefs, or decisions? Surely there is nothing wrong with empathizing with the character's decision or belief since a representation of a decision is not a decision, and the representation of a belief is not a belief. One can fully grasp a belief from the character's viewpoint without having the belief, and likewise for an intention or a decision.

But the moral objection is almost always raised against empathizing with an immoral sensation or emotion. To perfectly grasp a feeling is to perfectly grasp the way it feels. The empathetic grasp is in the imagination. One cannot grasp what it is like to see red without seeing red in the imagination, and one cannot grasp what someone's hate is like without grasping the way their hate feels in the imagination. In Chapter 3 I wrote that the temptation to say that God feels what we feel in an empathetic state rests on the empiricist principle that an imaginary feeling is a copy of an actual sensation or feeling, which comes first. Hume argued that what he calls impressions come into the mind first, and the only phenomenal difference between an impression and an idea is its vivacity. He writes:

> Those perceptions, which enter with most force and violence, we may name *impressions*; and under this name I comprehend all our sensations, passions, and emotions, as they make their first appearance in the soul. By *ideas* I mean the faint images of these in thinking and reasoning. (Hume [1739] 2000, 1)

Since Hume argues that all the perceptions of the human mind are in one of these two categories, it follows that an empathetic state differs from an experiential impression only in the intensity of the state. But suppose that an idea is a perfect copy of an impression. Using Hume's reasoning, it seems to follow that the idea would be exactly the same as the impression. If so, a perfect phenomenal copy of a red sensation is a red sensation. A perfect phenomenal copy of a feeling of hate is a feeling of hate. A perfect empathizer would see red and feel hate. A perfect empathizer would have morally bad feelings, if there are any.

We can think of many more examples. Suppose a person feels fury or envy, or takes pleasure in the pain of another. Suppose a person feels so bitter about life that he wants to destroy the world.

Wouldn't it be morally wrong for a perfectly empathetic being to adopt those states empathetically in his imagination?

I think the answer is no, even for humans, but to explain why I think so, let's return to reading a novel or watching a movie. Often in films there is no attempt by the scriptwriter or actor to see inside the mind of the villainous character and reveal it to the audience from the villain's point of view. Once we see their evil actions, we dismiss them as undeserving of empathy. For instance, the movie *Schindler's List* portrays Amon Göth, the depraved SS officer who ran the Płaszów concentration camp during World War II. Ralph Fiennes gives a superb portrayal of Göth as a monster whose morning routine included executing Jews at random from his balcony. But Göth was a real person, and there must have been much in his consciousness that we do not see in the movie, presumably because he is beneath our attention, although not beneath the attention of God.

An example I have discussed in previous work is the character of Daniel Plainview, played by Daniel Day-Lewis in Paul Thomas Anderson's movie, *There Will Be Blood*.[12] Assuming you can tolerate watching this movie and can bring yourself to empathize with Daniel Plainview, you project yourself into the consciousness of a person who fears love and humiliates people who love him, who has no appreciation for the value of other persons, who enjoys inflicting pain, and is treacherous, prideful, and greedy. When you do that, you grasp the world and Plainview's reactions to the world through his eyes, but you also respond to those attitudes and feelings as yourself. If you have a negative reaction to cruelty, greed, and hate, you will have a negative reaction to your empathetic copy of those psychic states. You understand what it feels like to be hateful and greedy, but that does not make you hateful and greedy or even

---

[12] This character is loosely based on the character of James Arnold Ross, the father in Upton Sinclair's novel, *Oil*. The father in *Oil* is not the main character of the novel, and he is not as bad as the Daniel Day-Lewis character in the movie. The latter is unremittingly horrible, whereas the former has some redeeming features.

more likely to be hateful and greedy. In fact, it probably makes you less likely to be hateful and greedy. Since Plainview enjoys hurting people, empathizing with him will permit you to get what it feels like to enjoy hurting people, and I imagine you will feel revulsion for that also. Of course, it can happen that empathizing with another person in the real or fictional world leads you to change your reaction to certain psychic states. You might even come to judge that someone's feelings are not bad after all. If such a judgment is correct, it is no objection to the morality of empathizing with them. If it is incorrect, that is because you, the empathizer, have made a mistake in your reaction to the psychic state with which you are empathizing, but that is no objection to the empathetic state. It is a problem with the reaction that you have as the empathizer. Since God does not make mistakes in his responses to states with which he empathizes, there is no danger that empathizing with a hateful person is a taint on God's character, any more than it must be a taint on your character if you empathize with an evil character in a movie.

Unlike sensations, emotions have intentional objects. I am afraid *of* something, hope *for* something, feel disgusted *at* something, love someone, and so on. Empathizing with an emotion does not make the empathizer adopt the intentional object of the subject's emotion, as I mentioned in Chapter 3. Empathizing with delight at a person's suffering is not delight in their suffering. Empathizing with abhorrence of immigrants is not abhorrence of immigrants. But besides having an intentional object, I believe that an emotion also has a feeling component.[13] Fear, hatred, love, disgust—all emotions—feel a certain way apart from their cognitive content. Since the way an emotion feels is part of what it is, God's grasp of the feeling component of an emotion means that God grasps the way the feeling feels. God grasps it in his imagination. As I have

---

[13] I explain and defend an account of emotion as a state with both a cognitive component and an affective component in Zagzebski (2003) and Zagzebski (2004, ch. 2).

said, we often have feelings when we empathize, but that is because of features of human psychology that do not apply to the creator of the feelings. God is able to imaginatively grasp what our feelings are like because they preexisted in his imagination, and his consciousness is attached to them when they become actual. God is the First Cause and conserver of a state of hate. God has a perfect grasp of the state of hate. Given that God permits hate to exist for his own reasons, and given that nothing exists without God's will to conserve it, it must be acceptable to him to continually grasp a state of hate while he is conserving it in existence. How, then, can it be wrong of God to do so?

Suppose that your child hated another person. If you empathized with that hatred, you would know what the hatred feels like in your imaginative reconstruction of your child's state, and you would have many thoughts and emotions directed toward it. I imagine that you would feel sad and disappointed, eager to understand where the hate comes from, and hopeful that your child could be delivered from it. If you were a perfect empathizer, you would indeed grasp how hatred feels and you would hate it. That does not strike me as a bad thing. How can God hate evil without fully grasping it? How can God know *what* to hate or heal or forgive unless he grasps it perfectly? I have said that grasping it perfectly is not feeling it, but grasping it perfectly means that nothing in the person's experience is missing from the divine imagination.

That means that God must not only grasp what the feeling feels like, God must also grasp the context. If somebody takes pleasure in the suffering of another, God not only grasps the way the pleasure feels, but God also grasps the cause of the feeling and the experiences that led to it. Is there anything wrong with that? You grasp the entire context when you are watching a movie, and unless you are especially impressionable, you are not moved to become evil yourself.

This answer will not satisfy someone who insists that God cannot be conscious of someone's intrinsically immoral state

of consciousness even though God does not himself hate anyone or enjoy the suffering of others. On this view, God would be
contaminated by his own creatures if he really grasped what it is like
to have their bad feelings in the context in which they feel them.
A perfectly good God must be shielded from too intimate a contact
with certain human experiences.

I find the idea that God would be less than perfect, and hence,
less than divine if he had too close a contact with the created world
quite implausible, but I doubt that this issue can be settled without
a closer look at other Christian doctrines pertaining to the relationship between God and human beings, such as the doctrines
of grace, providence, and sanctification. Is anybody beneath God's
notice? Does God exercise his providence over the evil as well as
the good? Would God make any effort to sanctify the evildoers? It
seems to me that a perfect grasp of their subjectivity would be even
more important than the grasp of the subjectivity of good people.

The holiness objection is related to the moral objection. This is
the objection that there are conscious human states that are not immoral, but are opposed to holiness, and it would be demeaning for
God to have too close a contact with them. Ryan Mullins (2020b)
calls this "the problem of creepy emotions."[14] Sexual feelings would
be an example. This is an interesting objection because it immediately raises the question of what holiness is and how the holy relates
to human beings. Holiness is not often mentioned in the New
Testament, but there are many references to the holiness of Yahweh
in the Hebrew Scriptures. "Holy, holy, holy is the Lord of hosts; the
whole earth is full of his glory" (Isa. 6:3 NRSV). Holiness is a quality
unique to Yahweh, although creatures can be holy in a derived form
by contact with God.

Rudolf Otto's (1958) analysis of holiness has been highly influential, and many people identify with the distinctively religious

---

[14] Mullins (2020b) includes both immoral emotions and feelings that are not immoral
but are inappropriate to a divine being under the heading of "creepy emotions."

emotion and the distinctively religious object he describes. For Otto, holiness is what he calls the numinous, a mysterious divine quality of being wholly other, and which is both fearful and fascinating to humans. The human being feels unworthy to even stand close to the holy, and distance is respected in ritual consecration, sacred objects, altars, and vestments—all of which are treated with reverence.

The holy contrasts with the profane. The profane is not the same as the immoral; it is the opposite of the lofty and the sacred. When we treat objects as sacred, we intentionally separate them from the profane, which includes ordinary objects, and especially anything associated with our so-called lower nature such as menstrual blood. The holy is exalted above ordinary human life, although objects used in worship are holy, and profane objects can be made holy by contact with them.

With this conception of the holy, we can see why it is natural to think that it would be unworthy of the one holy God to empathize or perceive or otherwise perfectly grasp subjective states like human sexual desire or an animal's delight in making a kill. But I think that these examples are not really in a special class because everything in creaturely existence is profane in the sense we have inherited from the Hebrew Scriptures. But when I have heard this objection, the assumption was that some parts of human life are more profane than others. As Mullins (2020b) puts it, some of it is "creepy." Is God's perfect grasp of the creepy compatible with his holiness?

It is surely mistaken to think that God can be contaminated by his creation, but perhaps we feel more comfortable if God remains above us and does not get too close to our daily lives because the religious urge is the urge to get above our daily lives. We hope to rise to the level of contact with the divine; we do not want God to sink to the level of the profane. I think, though, that it is significant that in the Hebrew scriptures, contact between a holy object and a profane one sanctifies the profane, but the holy one does not lose its holiness.

> And you shall make of these a sacred anointing oil blended as by the perfumer; it shall be a holy anointing oil. With it you shall anoint the tent of meeting and the ark of the covenant, and the table and all its utensils, and the lampstand and its utensils and the altar of incense, and the altar of burnt offering with all its utensils, and the basin with its stand; you shall consecrate them so that they may be most holy; whatever touches them will become holy. (Exod. 30:25–29, NRSV)

Notice that the scripture does not say that the basin and utensils make the holy oil profane. Rather, the holy oil makes the basin and utensils and all the other objects it touches holy. I interpret that to mean that the holy is never corrupted, contaminated or diminished by anything profane. If God is supremely holy, God is never contaminated by close contact with the profane, even the creepy profane.

Mullins (2020b) argues that empathy with creepy feelings is a problem for a passibilist like himself, and he offers two responses to the problem. The first one uses my previously published views about divine empathy. The second one is what he calls the maximal God option. Borrowing from a point made by Yujin Nagasawa (2017, 92), he argues that perfect-being theology need not be committed to the omni-God thesis, but it can affirm the maximal God thesis according to which God has the maximally consistent set of power, knowledge, and goodness (Mullins 2020b, 12). The passibilist can say that perfect omnisubjectivity is inconsistent with God's moral perfection or rationality, and therefore God does not have a perfect grasp of all conscious states because some of them are irrational or immoral or creepy. But God can still have maximal empathy even if not perfect omnisubjectivity. On this approach, God's empathy is in the degree maximally consistent with God's moral and rational perfection.

The idea that perfect-being theology may need to modify what is intended in the omni-God thesis is understandable, but notice that there is more than one way in which the attributes of God can be consistent with each other in a maximally perfect deity. If holiness is incompatible with omnisubjectivity, and omnisubjectivity is entailed by perfect knowledge, we must be mistaken about one of the attributes, but which one? Maximal consistency can mean that God does not have perfect empathy, as Mullins suggests in his second option, or maximal consistency can mean that God has perfect empathy, but he is not perfectly holy or good as defined by a previous understanding of those attributes.

I proposed my own modification of the omni-God thesis in *Divine Motivation Theory* (2004, ch. 7). I wrote that book before I got the idea of omnisubjectivity, and I did not think of the way it connects with omnisubjectivity until I read Mullins' second proposal. I have argued that omnisubjectivity is compatible with divine goodness and holiness without modifying the omni-God thesis, but the modification of that thesis is another way to answer the objections of this section. In that book I suggested that God's motives are ontologically primary; individual perfections are ontologically secondary. The way to understand the consistency of the divine perfections with each other is to define each one as the possession of the relevant perfection in the degree God is motivated to possess. Perfect goodness is what God is motivated to be or do. Perfect knowledge is knowledge in the kind and degree God is motivated to have. Perfect power is power in the kind and degree God is motivated to have. All perfections derive from God's motives. If God is motivated to be omnisubjective, that is good because goodness is just what God is motivated to be. The compatibility of omnisubjectivity with goodness and holiness follows from the thesis that goodness and holiness are not independently defined properties, but rather are properties derivative from God's motives.

Some readers may want to say that God is motivated to refrain from being perfectly omnisubjective because some of our conscious states are beneath him, but I think that what we consider to be states appropriate for God needs to be reconsidered. Some of our reactions are due more to our own feelings about ordinary human life than feelings about God. If some readers are sure that God should not grasp our sexual feelings, I doubt that there is anything I can say. However, I think that it is important to consider the fact that the Creator invented sex and if we believe in divine conservation, that means that if God stopped paying attention to us for even an instant, we would go out of existence. So, we should be happy for the attention.

That brings up a related objection that focuses not on what grasping human feelings does to God, but on what it does to us. The complaint is that God should not observe our sexual feelings or other states that we consider to be especially private. The problem is not that the feelings are creepy, but that God would be creepy if he observed them. God seems like a peeping Tom. If that is the image we have, I think it means that we are using the wrong image. God does not peer at us; God is within us. If consciousness flows out of God with God's own consciousness attached to it, God keeps our consciousness in existence.

It is significant that even apart from omnisubjectivity, traditional Christians believe that we cannot hide anything from God, and I gave some scripture references to support that position in Chapter 2. It does not go much further, and perhaps no further at all, to say that every one of our conscious states is open to God in its entirety, not only as propositional knowledge. If this consequence of omnisubjectivity is problematic, other Christian teachings are also problematic, including the exhaustive knowledge God has of us in the last judgment. I do not see how the intimate relation between God and the created universe can jeopardize God's nature or in any way sully his sacredness. Human and animal creatures are lowly in one way and magnificent in another. If the created world was not magnificent, God would not have created it.

4.5. Can an Essentially Infinite Deity Grasp States of Finite Creatures?

Divine consciousness is infinitely expansive. God can grasp everything in the universe he created, including all the feelings within it. Since God created subjects of experience, God grasps the subject having the experience. God grasps the subject having the experience in his or her own unique way. The way we experience things is essentially different from the way God experiences things, but God can know how we experience things because he made us the way we are.

I have mentioned the empiricist assumption that what we imagine depends upon previous experience. Imagining fear depends upon the previous experience of fear. Imagining confusion depends upon the previous experience of confusion. Since God is the creator of feelings, this principle cannot apply to God, but even if God does not have to have an experience in order to imagine what that experience is like, can God imagine experiential states that are impossible for him to have? It is contrary to God's nature to experience fear, bewilderment, confusion, surprise, and many other human subjective states. Therefore, it can be argued, God cannot imagine what it is like to be in those states.

I think that this objection can be answered even with a close analogy to our own imagination when we empathize. As I said in Chapter 3, when I empathize, I do not imagine that I (LZ) am identical with my friend Pat, or a man, or a dog, or a character in a novel. I do not imagine an impossible identity. What I do is to imagine that I am not my actual self, but that Pat or a man or a dog is myself, and I imagine having their feelings, feelings that I do not have, and which might even be inconsistent with my nature. So, I propose that God does not imagine himself being bewildered or afraid. Rather, he imagines being me and being bewildered. He imagines being a dog who is afraid. That possibility is no different than imagining having senses and smelling roses.

But the objection could be pressed farther. If God is essentially omniscient, maybe God cannot imagine *anybody* being confused or bewildered. Any state inconsistent with God's nature is out of reach of his imagination. When I think I am imagining being a dog, I am not really doing so. I am only imagining what a human thinks a dog's consciousness would be like. I really cannot imagine anything inconsistent with human nature, and similarly, God cannot really imagine anything inconsistent with divine nature. So, God cannot imagine what it is like to be bewildered or confused or fearful.

I think that this argument is mistaken, but I also think that the empathy model is probably insufficient to show why God has no difficulty in imagining confusion and fear. We must return to the point that as the Creator, God knows exactly what he created in all details. If so, he must know what it is like to be ignorant and stupid and fearful and confused. He knows what it is like to have false beliefs and feelings based on those beliefs. He knows what it is like to be a finite creature, the kind of creature he decided to create.

I have argued that God does not have to rely upon his own experiences or even experiences he could have had in order to know what having a human experience is like. Divine empathy is not like our empathy. That is both an advantage and a disadvantage of the empathy model. When we imagine God's empathy as like ours, it seems to depend upon his own experience. If it does not depend upon his own experience, the analogy with empathy is weaker. But I also think that empathy is only one activity of the imagination. We can imagine a feeling without empathizing, and God surely is able to do that. I think that all possible conscious states must be contained in God's imagination prior to the creation, before any creatures exist with whom he will empathize. I will turn to that in the next chapter.

In this chapter I have examined arguments that God either cannot or should not fully grasp certain conscious states as they are experienced by human creatures. I realize that some readers take these objections more seriously than others, but I believe that the objections can be answered in a way that will satisfy most Christian theists. I think that the same responses should satisfy Muslims and Jews, but I will leave it to their scholars to respond to these objections if they otherwise accept the omnisubjectivity of God.

5

Counteractual Subjectivity

5.1. Grasping Counteractual Subjectivity

Does the domain of subjectivity extend beyond the actual world? If
so, does an omnisubjective God grasp subjective states that do not
exist in the actual world but exist in other possible worlds? Do such
states even make sense? Suppose Mary never leaves her black-and-
white room during her entire life. Does God know what it *would*
be like for Mary to see color? What if Mary was never born? Would
God know what it would be like if Mary came into the world, spent
much of her life in a black-and-white room, and then saw color for
the first time?

I will use the term "counteractual" rather than "counterfactual" to
refer to possible but nonactual subjective states because "counterfactual" means "contrary to fact." If a fact is a true proposition, and if
I am right that the content of a subjective state does not correspond
to a proposition, it misses the point to say that counteractual subjective states are contrary to facts. Counteractual subjective states
are not actual, but if they were actual, they would be the same kind
of phenomenon as actual subjective states, and if actual subjective
states do not correspond to propositions, neither do counteractual
subjective states. In standard modal metaphysics, maximal consistent possibilities are constituted by sets of propositions, or possible worlds. We have already seen problems with the discourse of
possible worlds if we take the existence of subjectivity seriously. We
are now about to encounter further problems. Even if God knows
which propositions are true in each possible world, that may not
be enough for perfect knowledge of the realm of possibility for the

Omnisubjectivity. Linda Trinkaus Zagzebski, Oxford University Press. © Oxford University Press 2023.
DOI: 10.1093/oso/9780197682098.003.0005

same reason that knowledge of which propositions are true in the actual world is not enough for perfect knowledge of the realm of actuality. In this chapter I will investigate whether God grasps subjective states in other possible worlds, what it would mean for there to be such states, and how the grasp of such states is related to the grasp of actual subjective states and objective states of affairs.

If there are possible subjective states that are not actual, there are strong reasons to think that the grasp of those states is required by cognitive perfection. In Chapter 1 I argued that if God grasps what it is like for Mary to see red, he has a more extensive grasp of his creation than if he merely knows the propositional fact that Mary sees red. Similarly, if God grasps what it would be like for Mary to have any conscious state that she could have, and furthermore, what it would be like for any possible conscious being to have any conscious state possible for that being, God has a more extensive grasp of the realm of possibilities than if he merely knows which propositions are possibly true. If some other possible world containing conscious beings were actual, that world would contain first-person subjective experiences. Lacking a grasp of those experiences as they would be experienced by individual beings in that world would be a failure to fully grasp that world, and hence, it would be an imperfection in God's grasp of possibilities.

Divine knowledge of counteractual subjectivity is also implied by religious practice, particularly personal prayer. Sometimes people who face a life-changing decision and who are having trouble making up their mind pray about it because they believe that God knows what it would be like for them to marry a certain person, move to a different city, take a new job, or do any of the other things that have far-reaching consequences that they cannot foresee. They assume that God grasps their possible subjective states, and God might use this knowledge to help them make a decision through prayer.

The ability to grasp counteractual conscious states from a first-person perspective is probably also a condition for ideal creative power. If God does not know what it would be like for conscious beings to have their experiences, how can God know what to create? He would not know everything relevant to the creation of a world unless his omnisubjectivity extends to a complete grasp of the first-person conscious states of all conscious beings in that world. He would not know what it would be like if that world were actual, and so he would not be able to compare what it would be like if one world were actual rather than another.[1] He would not know which world he prefers if some of the most important features of a world (arguably, all the most important features) are outside his conscious grasp. His creative choice would be very risky.[2]

Theists who adopt possible worlds discourse agree that God knows all the facts in every possible world. If so, God knows the fact that there is a certain amount of good and evil in a world and the fact that there are certain pains, preferences, desires, fears, cries of distress, enjoyments, loving relationships, and all the other states of subjective experience in each world. These facts are abstractions. A failure to grasp the subjective experiences that ground them is a failure to fully grasp the world that contains them. In addition, if God does not know what counteractual experiences are like, that not only puts limitations on God as creator, it limits his knowledge of his own counteractual self.

There are further practical problems that ensue if God's omnisubjectivity does not extend to other worlds. Presumably, God's interaction with the world does not end with the creation. God might intervene in temporal events, and he might act in ways that involve reward and punishment, either during a person's

---

[1] I thank Timothy Miller for pressing this point in conversation many years ago, and for helpful recent exchanges about counteractual subjectivity.

[2] I am not suggesting that God directly creates an entire possible world, including all the subjective states in that world. I have proposed in other work (Zagzebski 1991, ch. 5) that God creates a world-germ, permitting free creatures to contribute to the actualization of the world. That idea complicates my point, but it is still the case that God would take unnecessary risks unless he knows what subjective states would follow from his creative act, and what subjective states would follow from alternative creative acts.

lifetime or at the end of it. If God does not know in advance what it would be like for persons to have different possible subjective experiences, including experiences of joy and suffering, his plan for rewarding or punishing those persons lacks the crucial feature of knowing the precise outcome of alternative plans.

Some philosophers believe that the future of the actual world is ontologically in the same category as the merely possible but nonactual. There is no actual future to be known, only an infinite number of possible futures. For those philosophers, the topic of this chapter applies to the future as well as to other possible worlds, but I will leave it to them to draw the relevant conclusions from my arguments.

If we accept the position that God grasps nonactual but possible subjectivity, as well as past and future subjectivity, we will need to amend the definition of omnisubjectivity:

> Omnisubjectivity is the property of having a complete and perfect grasp of all actual and possible subjective states, past, present, and future, from the first-person perspective of the possessor of the state.

If the grasp of counteractual subjectivity is a kind of knowledge, an expanded definition of omniscience would be required:

> Omniscience is the complete knowledge of all possible and actual subjective states as well as all possible and actual states of affairs objectively described.

A cognitively perfect being would need to have knowledge in this sense whether or not it is required by omniscience.

The metaphysical status of counteractual subjective states is related to the metaphysical status of counteractual persons such as fictional characters, and it is problematic for similar reasons. Fictional characters are interesting because they do not exist in the usual sense of exist, yet they live lives and have experiences that we can share in a way that is comparable to the way we share in the lives of other persons. In fact, a good novelist or filmmaker can make the subjectivity of a fictional character so realistic that fiction and film have become two of the most important forms of intersubjective experience. This is not an aberration. Fiction permits the reader or viewer to enter the lives of people very different from any person they will ever meet, and so it extends the reach of our comprehension of the subjectivity of others well beyond what we would be able to do in living our ordinary lives. But how can one of the primary examples of our grasp of the subjectivity of another be a grasp of the nonexistent? Fictional characters exist in our imagination. Can we conclude that they exist in the domain of possibility? Fictional characters reveal the obscurity of the relation between the actual and the merely possible. What is hard to deny is that the importance of subjectivity goes beyond what is actual.

Fictional characters blur the boundary between the possible and the actual because they are not actual beings, but they affect the actual world. There is also a fuzzy boundary between the fictional and the actual. Historical fiction features real people who lived in the past, but some of the incidents involving them are invented. Examples would be Gore Vidal's historical novels such as *Lincoln* (1984) and *Creation* (1981). The former is about Abraham Lincoln; the latter features Herodotus, Socrates, Confucius, and the Buddha, as well as other historical figures. Each is a blend of the historical and the fictional. That has led some writers to argue that historical characters in fiction should be classified as special fictional entities.[3] Presumably, what is special about them is that they combine the actual and the imaginary, so they have mixed metaphysical status, yet they have the narrative coherence of a single person. I think that this is an important point because our own narrative

---

[3] This view has recently gained some popularity. See, for example, Bonomi (2008), Voltolini (2013), and Motoarca (2014).

coherence includes imaginary events in our lives, events that are possible but never will be actual.

Our imaginations exist in the actual world. What we are imagining does not—or does it? What we imagine exists within our imagination. Does it also exist in some other possible world? One reason to think so is that one of our motives for imagining is to think of possibilities, and one of our tests for the fact that something is possible is that it is imaginable. We want to know what is possible and to think about what would happen if the merely possible were actual. Of course, sometimes what we imagine does not make sense, but when it does, we think that what we imagine is a possible being or state of affairs.

The imaginary affects the actual. The imaginary *is* actual in its status of the imaginary in the actual world. *What* we imagine might or might not exist in the actual world. Sometimes we imagine something actual in the past or future, and sometimes we imagine something in other possible worlds. We are able to imagine possibilities, and when we do, the actual world changes.

Imagination connects the possible and the actual, and causes responses in us. We admire Sherlock Holmes. We find Huckleberry Finn funny. We abhor the wicked witches in *Wizard of Oz*.[4] When we find a fictional situation funny and laugh out loud, our imagination of the nonactual situation causes an actual feeling that causes an overt action. So, there are connections between a possible being in a counterfactual situation, an actual subjective state, and an actual objective event. This point is even more obvious when what we are imagining is a different possible self. Our imaginary self affects our actual self. We would have a different actual self if

---

[4] The so-called paradox of emotional response to fiction appears in the philosophical literature on fiction and imagination. The puzzle arises from the conjunction of three mutually inconsistent statements: (1) People experience genuine emotions toward fictional characters and situations. (2) People do not believe in the existence of fictional characters or situations. (3) People do not experience genuine emotions when they do not believe in the existence of the objects of emotion. I reject (3). See Friend (2016) for a discussion of approaches to this problem.

our imagination of different counteractual selves went in a different direction. Our imaginings shape the direction of our lives. The possible but nonactual does not exist, and what does not exist cannot causally interact with the actual, but when we imagine the possible, we are not imagining nothing. The relation of intentionality connects our minds and the possible. When our minds grasp the merely possible, that grasp has effects in the actual world. The mind's directedness toward something that does not exist causally interacts with the actual world.

Think also about the ontological status of dreams. Like fiction, dreams are imaginary states of affairs, but unlike fiction, they are not imagined on purpose. Waking life affects dreams, and dreams affect waking life, so if the life in dreams is a possible life (when it makes sense), there is interaction between our representation of the possible and the actual. But the line between waking states and dream states is also vague. When I am falling asleep, I gradually go from waking memories, words, and images to dream images, and there is a short period of time when they occur at the same time.[5] Does another possible world intersect with the actual world in a dream? I am not suggesting that another possible world moves into the actual world when we dream. If it did, it would be actual. What I am suggesting is that our imaginative grasp of another possible world does enter the actual world. But how do we divide the two? The idea that there are distinct possible worlds has much theoretical power, but possible worlds discourse does not acknowledge the way that the possible and the actual are connected in the imagination and the fine and fluid line between them. In addition, it does not acknowledge the way that the imaginary affects objective events.

If God is omnisubjective, God knows imaginary subjective states in the actual world as we imagine them. The objects of those

---

[5] I recommend that you do not analyze this while it is happening since I can say from personal experience that it will keep you awake.

states are important because it is plausible to think that we are able to imagine them because they exist in other possible worlds. There are Huck Finns in other possible worlds. There are Sherlock Holmeses in other possible worlds.[6] Your counteractual selves exist in other possible worlds. Coherent dream events exist in other possible worlds. If so, God can grasp some counteractual beings and counteractual states of actual beings. But nobody would think that God's grasp of the counteractual depends upon the human imagination and dream life. Surely, if we can imagine some nonactual beings and nonactual states of actual beings, God can imagine all of them.

The status of nonactual beings with subjectivity is relevant to the models of the way God grasps creaturely subjectivity that I proposed in Chapter 3. Those models were designed to explain the way God grasps actual subjectivity, most naturally interpreted as occurrent subjective states. It is usually assumed that God knows the possible in a different way than the actual, so if we think that there is counteractual subjectivity, we will need to address the way God knows it. But the issue is more complicated than it seems if we also think that the imagination blurs the distinction between the actual and the merely possible, and that there are causal connections between our imaginative representations of the nonactual and actual events.

Aquinas makes a sharp distinction between the way God knows the merely possible and the way he knows the actual:

> Now a certain difference is to be noted in the consideration of those things that are not actual. For though some of them may not be in act now, still they were, or they will be; and God is said to know all these things with the knowledge of vision: for since God's act of understanding, which is His being, is measured by

---

[6] These reflections commit me to possibilism about fictional entities. I will address the problem of the indeterminacy of possible individuals in the next section.

eternity; and since eternity is without succession, comprehending all time, the present glance of God extends over all time, and to all things which exist in any time, as to objects present to Him. But there are other things in God's power, or the creature's, which nevertheless are not, nor will be, nor were; and as regards these He is said to have knowledge, not of vision, but of simple intelligence. (*ST* I q. 14.a. 9 corpus)

This passage distinguishes the way God knows what is actual at any point in time from the way God knows the merely possible but nonactual. God knows the actual, including the past and future, by a form of vision; God knows the merely possible by what Aquinas calls "simple intelligence." If I am right about the nature of subjectivity, God cannot know counteractual subjective states by simple intelligence, and as I have said, there is not a sharp line separating actual and counteractual in the imagination. If there is not a precise line between them, it is unlikely that there is a precise line in the way God knows them. Counteractual persons are similar to fictional characters. Sometimes the protagonist in a novel is the author's alternate self. Each of your counteractual selves is like a character you could be in a historical novel written a hundred years from now and featuring you. If God knows your counteractual self, it cannot be exactly the way he knows your actual self. God must know the actual as actual, and the merely possible as possible, but we need an explanation of how God grasps the difference, given that the difference is blurred, and given that some beings are partly actual and partly counteractual. The human imagination can combine the actual and the counteractual into the narrative coherence of a single person in historical fiction, and similarly, we combine our actual and counteractual selves in imaginary events that affect our actual future. I conclude that God's grasp of the possible cannot be as sharply divided from his grasp of the actual as Aquinas thought.

The metaphysical status of possible but nonactual worlds is contentious. The metaphysical status of counteractual subjectivity should be even more so. Fiction, dreams, and imagination illustrate the intimate connections between counteractual and actual subjective states. I have also mentioned connections between counteractual subjective states and objective states of affairs, as when we laugh at a fictional character's predicament. We need to keep these connections in mind as we examine whether and how God grasps counteractual subjective states.

5.2. The Status of Counteractual Subjectivity

Do we know that there is any such thing as counteractual subjectivity? How can a fictional character or your counteractual self have subjectivity? *What* being possesses the subjectivity? It goes without saying that a fictional character exists in the mind of the author, but when people talk about Sherlock Holmes, they are not talking about Conan Doyle. They are talking about Sherlock Holmes. Is Sherlock Holmes himself real in whatever sense it takes for him to have consciousness from the inside? Is there any inside to a fictional character?

When we reflect on our own counteractual selves, do we know what we are doing? We all imagine alternate lives for ourselves, lives in which we took paths we did not take, did things we did not do, met people we never met. What would it be like if I designed an outlandish house and started writing decorating books? I think I can imagine that up to a point, but the point at which my imagination fades comes pretty quickly. When we think about subjective experiences that will never be actual, are we sure that there is something that we are thinking about, and that there is something there that we could, in principle, think about even when our imagination fades away?

Both our past and our future could be (could have been) different, and those lives would be just as rich in subjective states as our actual life. But we could be mistaken about that. Perhaps when we think about possible but nonactual subjective states in the past or future, and when we think about the subjective states of nonactual beings, there is nothing to think about that is as determinate as actual subjective states. Suppose I describe to you an imaginary person who comes to your door, speaks to you, and gives you a gift. I describe the person carefully and relate an amusing imaginary exchange. Surely, if I intend to talk about a possible individual, there is an infinite number of them fitting that description. There is no single possible person who satisfies the description in my imagination and yours. But arguably, that problem is solvable because it is due to a limitation on our imaginations, not on the specificity of possible circumstances. Most philosophers believe that a possible state of affairs is determinate in principle, corresponding to a particular proposition, and it would be actual if a world containing that state of affairs were actual. We might not be able to refer to a single possible individual in our imagination, and the novelist or screen writer might not be able to refer to one possible being over another with the same properties. There might not, then, be such a thing as what Sherlock would feel if he stepped foot in New Mexico because one possible Sherlock would feel one thing and another possible Sherlock would feel something else. On this interpretation, "Sherlock Holmes" is not a proper name of a unique possible individual, and so there is no single set of subjective experiences he possesses. But that is not a denial of possible but nonactual subjectivities for Sherlock. It just means that there are too many of them for us to refer to one in particular. The Sherlock we imagine and that Conan Doyle imagines might correspond to a set of possible individuals.[7]

_____

[7] Saül Kripke (1972/1980) argues that we cannot identify a fictional entity with a merely possible entity, for suppose that we discovered a man in the actual world who is just like Sherlock Holmes. That man would not be the Sherlock Holmes of Doyle's narratives because that man is not a fictional character, and he is not causally connected to Doyle. For the same reason, no person in another possible world can be Sherlock because that possible person (or persons) is not fictional in the worlds in which he exists, and Conan Doyle is not causally connected to them. Kripke says that when we speak of

In the case of an actual being like yourself, the problem of Sherlock does not arise since you have a determinate set of properties that necessarily apply to you and only to you. There is only one of you. You can be in a variety of counterfactual situations, and as long as the situations are determinate in principle, I see no objection to the idea that there is such a thing as what you would feel like in those circumstances on the grounds of indeterminacy. But followers of the literature on Middle Knowledge will notice another issue. Even if there is such a thing as what it would feel like if you were in some counterfactual situation, is there any such thing as what you would choose to do in that situation? Suppose that you have never jumped from an airplane. You might wonder what it would be like if you did. And you might wonder if you would choose to do it again. The answer could easily be maybe, but maybe not. There are numerous possible worlds in which you jump from an airplane, but perhaps you choose to jump again in one world, and you choose not to in another world, and the two worlds are equidistant from the actual world. If so, since choosing is a subjective event, there is no such thing as what your subjective state of choosing *would* be like, only that it might be one way and it might be another. But again, this is not a problem for the existence of counteractual subjectivity or God's knowledge of it. It would mean that God knows that in certain counterfactual circumstances certain subjective states would exist. In other counterfactual circumstances, certain subjective states might exist, but they might not, and God could distinguish the worlds in which the states exist from those in which they do not.

Sherlock, we pretend to assert propositions (see Kripke 2013, esp. 40–42). I agree that we cannot be causally connected to nonexistent objects, but we can intend to refer to possible beings. Fictional characters correspond to more than one possible individual. There is no difficulty in the position that fictional characters are possible beings, but there is more than one of them. There is more than one Sherlock. I also think that being fictional is not an essential property of any possible Sherlock. It is a contingent fact about Conan Doyle and all possible Sherlocks that Conan Doyle thought of them.

In my first paper on omnisubjectivity (Zagzebski 2008), I ended with the speculation that only the actual world contains subjective states. My reason was that there is a puzzle about what actuality is that is solved if there are no counteractual subjective states, and if there are no counteractual subjective states, the actual world is clearly distinguishable from other possible worlds. Returning to the standard treatment of possible worlds, the only thing distinguishing the actual world from other possible worlds is that the actual world has the mysterious feature of actuality. Actuality is a peculiar property if it is a property at all. It is not a descriptive property since all possible worlds are fully describable without it. It is not contained in the exhaustive list of propositions distinguishing one world from another. We can look at possible worlds in as much detail as we wish, and we find actuality in none of them. The fact that this world is the actual one is independent of its exhaustive description in a set of propositions. On this line of reasoning, actuality is not a property instantiated in any possible world.

There is another way we could look at actuality. Each possible world is an exhaustive list of propositions that would be true if that world were actual. There are possible worlds in which humans can see ultraviolet colors. That is to say, if any of those worlds were actual, it would be true that humans see ultraviolet colors. Using the same reasoning, if any possible world were actual, it would be true that it is actual. According to this line of thought, actuality is a property instantiated in all possible worlds. If actuality is a property of all possible worlds or no possible worlds, actuality does not distinguish one world from another.

One answer to this problem is David Lewis's (1970) well-known indexical theory of actuality, according to which actuality is not absolute. Actuality for us is the realm that includes us, and in general, actuality for any being x is the realm that includes x. All possible worlds exist just as much as ours does, and each is actual relative to the beings in it. Lewis's theory is radical, but it is one way to explain why we do not find any property called actuality in our world that distinguishes it from all other worlds.

It has been more than fifty years since Lewis proposed his theory, and it led to numerous debates about the status of possible worlds and the relationship between the actual world and other possible worlds. Discussions generally assume that there is nothing special in the content of the actual world that distinguishes it from the content of other possible worlds, and that generates the problem of actuality. My conjecture in my first omnisubjectivity paper is that there *is* a difference in content. Only the actual world is concrete and alive. It alone has thoughts, feelings, and sensations. Only the actual world has conscious subjects because only the actual world exists. All other worlds are mere abstractions. They are bloodless and soulless. They are merely sets of propositions. They lack anything interior to consciousness; they merely include external descriptions of consciousness. The actual world is the real world. Everything else is merely ideas in minds.

I think now that we must reject this idea. We can think of possible worlds as sets of propositions, in which case the actual world is just as abstract as other possible worlds. But other possible worlds are alternate histories of the world. If some other possible world containing conscious beings had been actual, it would be just as concrete and alive, and would have subjectivity just as much as the actual world has. There is no reason to think that any such world would be any thinner in content than the world that actually exists. In addition, I have argued that the human imagination connects actual and counteractual subjectivity and the line between them is vague. When we think about our counteractual self, the actual and the possible blend and merge. When we read historical fiction, it would be odd to think that we move back and forth between the concrete life of an actual being and the abstract idea of being with no subjectivity. The life of a person in a work of historical fiction has the narrative coherence of a single person, yet it is partly actual and partly counteractual.

This problem arises from the fact that the discourse of possible worlds we have inherited forces us to make a sharp division between one world and another by the nature of the language we use to express propositions. Possible worlds are defined as distinct sets of maximally complete and consistent propositions that are mirrored in the language we use to express them. I have already argued that subjectivity is not fully captured in propositions. Now we see more problems with the view that all of modal reality is captured in possible worlds discourse. That discourse is blind to the many ways the actual and the possible connect through the intentionality of the human mind. I find something in real life funny and that causes me to imagine an even funnier possible person. I imagine something funny that does not exist in the actual world and that makes me laugh. I imagine something funny and that makes me see something else in the actual world as funny. There are not only connections between subjective states and objective facts, there are many objective facts that are grounded in subjective experience. The proposition expressed by "Linda thinks that is funny" is true because of the subjective experience that grounds it. Similarly, the proposition expressed by "Linda would find that funny if..." is true because there is a counteractual subjective state that grounds it.

It seems to me that we are not clear about the division between the actual and the counteractual. The actual exists and the merely possible does not, but the possible is not a nothing. When we imagine it we are not imagining nothing. There are logical and psychological connections between the actual and the counteractual, and between counteractual subjectivity and the truth of propositions in other possible worlds.

The intellect is not the best faculty for grasping all these connections. On the other hand, the imagination does it easily.

5.3. How Does God Grasp Counteractual Subjective States?

The models of omnisubjectivity in Chapter 3 were constructed to explain divine knowledge of actual subjectivity. If there is no such thing as counteractual subjectivity, we will not need to make any change or addition to those models. But as long as God knows counteractual subjective states, those models will need to be revisited, and we will need to keep in mind that the boundary between the actual and the counteractual is not precise.

Let us begin with the perceptual model. We can imagine God "seeing" the nonexistent, but the perceptual analogy is almost always built out of perceiving actual and occurrent events. In addition, we usually speak of perception to express our contact with something outside of us, but I doubt that it makes sense to think of God perceiving possible subjectivities as if they were outside of him. Those who believe that the entire realm of possibility exists independent of God in a Platonic heaven can adopt the perceptual model for the grasp of possibilities, but if the realm of the possible exists within God, the perceptual model is not appropriate. We could, of course, say that God sees the merely possible "in his mind's eye," but if so, his mind's eye would mostly plausibly be his imagination. According to this model, God would grasp the actual and the counteractual using two different faculties, and if the difference between them is vague, that issue would need to be addressed.

The empathy model has the advantage that it works as well for nonactual subjective states as for actual states. Empathy is located in the imagination, and it is an easy step to extend the model to say that God can empathize with the subjective states of nonactual beings for the same reason you can empathize with Don Quixote and Jane Austen's characters and many other fictional beings. Using this model, God grasps both actual and counteractual subjectivity the same way. The vague difference between the actual and the counteractual is not a problem. God can imagine the ways they connect, and if God's grasp of objective states of affairs is also in his imagination, he can easily grasp the causal interactions between subjective and objective states of affairs with the same faculty. If there is a vague line between the actual and the counteractual, God imagines it with a vague line.

I have thought of a worrisome feature about this model. One reason the empathy model is appealing is that it is comforting to believe that God is always with us. Divine empathy means that we are never alone in our suffering, and we are always sharing our joy. We can have a deep relationship with God. But suppose that God does exactly the same thing with somebody who does not even exist. Am I on the same level as a nonexistent being? And God's motive to empathize with a being who does not exist cannot have anything to do with loving them or sharing in their lives, so why would God do it? When we empathize with a fictional character, we do it for our own sake. If God empathized with a merely possible being, he cannot be doing it for his own sake, and there is no being for whose sake he would be empathizing. On the other hand, grasping the subjective states of nonactual beings in an empathetic way is just what a cognitively perfect being does. Even humans often let our imaginations wander to think about beings who will never exist without any particular motive. Women sometimes think with regret about all the babies we could have had but who will never exist. It is the regret that the possible is not the actual. How does God feel about nonactual persons? Does God regret that they are not actual? Does God care about them? If so, maybe all of them are actual. That would push us in the direction of the David Lewis approach to possible worlds. I will not pursue that line, but will leave it to those who have their own reasons for preferring that approach.

Panentheism needs an addition if there is possible but nonactual subjectivity, but I see no reason why the theory cannot be used in explaining the divine grasp of nonactual subjective states. If the created world is part of God but God transcends the creation, God can think and feel in the created world, but can also think and feel about other possibilities in his imagination. The issue of whether the divine imagination is separate from the created universe would need to be addressed, and the vague difference between the actual and the counteractual would also need to be addressed.

I have proposed that God grasps our actual subjective states in his imagination. The imagination is the faculty we use in grasping the subjective states of other persons, and the imagination is the most likely faculty for God's grasp of creaturely subjective states. The divine imagination has not received much attention from philosophers, but if we can speak of God seeing and thinking and willing, why not imagining? When we say God thinks and wills, we use the terms "thinks" and "wills" in a way that is analogous to their uses as applied to human faculties. In Aquinas's theory of analogous predication, God's thinking and willing are prior to our thinking and willing. God's thinking and willing cause our faculties to function, and our faculties are participations in the divine faculties. Similarly, I propose that God has an imagination in an analogous sense. Our imaginations participate in the divine imagination. What we do by imagining, God does more perfectly in the divine imagination. I propose that God grasps both counteractual subjectivity and actual subjectivity in his imagination.

What is a feeling in the divine imagination? I argued in Chapter 3 that grasping what it is like to have a certain feeling in the imagination is not the same as having the feeling. When we imagine something visual, we do not see what the image represents, but we know what it would be like if we saw it. We do not hear the song going through our head, but we know what it was like to hear it and what it would be like to hear it again. We do not feel the feeling in our imagination, but we know what it would be like if we had the feeling. We can confirm that we knew what the feeling would be like when we do have the feeling and can then say to ourselves, "Yes, that's what I thought it would be like." But I also said that I realize that some readers will say that perfectly grasping what a feeling is like in the imagination is the same as having the feeling. That position has a harder task in answering the moral objection discussed in the last chapter, but now we see another problem. If God felt all the feelings he grasps in his imagination, and all possible feelings are in his imagination, God would not only feel all actual feelings, he would feel all possible feelings! That is a striking consequence of the position that a perfect imaginative feeling is a feeling. It is interesting, but

I will not pursue it for the purposes of this book because it is too far from traditional Western theism.

The idea that God grasps all possible subjective states in his imagination is a simple and obvious extension of the empathy model, and it is consistent with all the models of omnisubjectivity I have proposed. This is important because when philosophers speak of the realm of possibility, they almost always think of it as objects of the intellect. That is true of medieval as well as contemporary philosophers, and that is why Aquinas proposed that God knows the realm of possibility through "simple intelligence." We inherited from the ancient Greeks the idea that anything we know nonexperientially is known through the intellect. There are only two faculties for getting knowledge: the senses and the intellect. When the imagination is mentioned in Western philosophy, it is usually in the context of poetry or art, and it is only in recent history that it has been interpreted as a faculty that has anything to do with attaining truth. Plato put the imagination in the lowest rank of human faculties, and in the *Republic*, he says that the poet and artist are imitators "at a third remove from the truth" (*Republic* X 602c). Aristotle placed the imagination between the senses (*to aesthetikon*) and the intellect (*nous*). He says that imagination, like memory, is an effect of perception, but the soul never thinks without an image (*De Anima* 431a 16). The imagination derives from perception, and it is an aid to the intellect. It does not have a primary function of its own.[8]

Contemporary accounts of the human imagination attribute many different functions to it, and it is not clear that they all fit within a single faculty.[9] For my purposes, there are two functions of the human imagination that apply to God. One is its representative

[8] See Casey (2000, introduction) for a historical survey of the problematic place of imagination in Western philosophy and psychology, esp. 14–19.

[9] Amy Kind (2013) examines four different contexts in which imagining has been assigned a central place: mindreading, pretense, engagement with fiction, and modal epistemology. She argues that no single mental activity can do all the explanatory work that has been assigned to imagining.

function in grasping the minds of actual or nonactual beings; the other is its productive function in creativity.

With due regard for the fact that we are not using the term "imagination" univocally when we compare the human and divine imaginations, we can say that the operation of imagining is distinct from the intellect's function of abstract thought. The intellect grasps sets of propositions and their relations. The intellect grasps possible worlds. That differs from imagining a state of affairs— picturing it as one would experience it if it were actual. Imagining a possible state of affairs and grasping a proposition expressing that state of affairs are two different things. They are two different ways of grasping the possible.

We might wonder if grasping a proposition and imagining the state of affairs it expresses really are different. George Berkeley apparently thought that there is no difference. If there are no abstract ideas, as Berkeley famously argued, grasping the proposition expressed by "There is an apple and two bananas in the fruit bowl" is just to imagine it. An intellectual grasp reduces to an event in the imagination. The imagination does the work. I doubt that Berkeley is right, but if he is, my point about the important function of the imagination is even stronger. I am not going to deny that the divine intellect has a function, but if God grasps all possibilities in his imagination, we can easily explain God's perfect grasp of possible subjective states and their relationship to actual subjective states as well as the relationship between possible and actual subjective states and objective states of affairs. God's imagination is a powerful faculty.

Brian Leftow (2012) has a more radical position. He argues that the source of the entire realm of the created modalities of possibility and necessity, whether objective or subjective, is the divine imagination.[10] He argues that there are no possible worlds or any

---

[10] Leftow does not use the terms "subjective" and "objective," but he discusses both God's creation of objective properties and God's creation of experiential states.

kind of abstract entity. Prior to the creation, God thinks up possible creatures in his imagination, and does so all at once in what Leftow calls "the Biggest Bang" (2012, ch. 10).[11] That includes objective properties like redness. He proposes that God spontaneously comes up with redness by a feat of imagination in which God invents the natures of things: "Red is a color because that is how God thinks of it. It is necessarily a color because He does not possibly think of it any other way" (Leftow 2012, 279). Leftow also tentatively proposes that God makes up experiential states such as pain the same way. Although he appears to be neutral on whether God feels pain, he says that even if God does not actually feel pain, he must be able to think up states that are phenomenally very close to pain (Leftow 2012, 285–286). The conclusion is that everything that exists or possibly exists apart from God comes out of the divine imagination.

I agree with Leftow that God creates out of his imagination, but I am neutral on whether Leftow is right that God makes the necessary necessary and the possible possible by imagining things a certain way. Leftow is thinking of the inventive function of God's imagination. Modalities are invented by God. God imagines red and imagines it as a color, and red is necessarily a color because that is how God imagines it. My proposal is more modest. The imagination is a faculty for grasping possible states of affairs even if the imagination does not make them possible. Imagination can be an inventive faculty, but it is also a faculty for empathy, mind-reading, and grasping objective possibilities. It is the only appropriate faculty for grasping subjective possibilities, and it is a faculty superior to the intellect for grasping objective possibilities.

To see why, consider any objective event or state of affairs you wish. As I look east in the early morning, I see the sun rising

[11] Leftow argues that God invents the modalities of the created world through his imagination, but that is not to say that God makes himself necessary by imagining himself that way. Divine necessity is independent of created modalities (ch. 17).

over the Sangre de Cristo mountains, one of my favorite sights. Allegedly, that event corresponds to a proposition expressed by something like "The sun is rising over the mountains east of Linda's house." Anybody can grasp that proposition and its logical and probabilistic connections with other propositions. Grasping that proposition is an act of the intellect. Assuming that Berkeley was mistaken, it differs from imagining the event, although, of course, grasping the proposition often leads to imagining the event. When we imagine an event, it can have greater or lesser detail, greater or lesser clarity. Imagining a situation comes in degrees. What is hard to deny is that imagining an event is a superior way of grasping it than merely understanding the proposition that expresses it, and the greater the imaginative clarity and detail, the better the grasp is. We can imagine the possible as if we were sensing it. That is why I propose that the imagination is a superior way to grasp states of affairs than the intellectual grasp of propositions.

A defender of the adequacy of propositional knowing might respond that the problem is in my example. The sentence I chose to express the proposition has a content that is exceedingly thin. A detailed sentential expression of my visual image would be very long, perhaps consisting of a conjunction of uncountably many sentences strung together. I think that this response makes my position even stronger. Each time we add another conjunct, or more adjectives and other descriptive words, we do so because we admit the insufficiency of the previous sentence. In Chapter 1 I argued that if our grasp of propositions is mediated through language, propositions cannot fully express subjective states. Even worse than the paucity of language is the fact that the nature of propositions is to be third-personal, so they never express first-person experience adequately. My argument here is that even the grasp of objective states of affairs is done more adequately by the imagination than by the intellectual grasp of propositions. There are obvious weaknesses in human imagination, but the imagination is the kind of faculty that grasps what is possible or what was actual in the past or what will be actual in the future in a way that is superior to the grasp of propositions by the intellect because, like memory, it mimics direct experience.

I find the hypothesis that God grasps all possibilities in his imagination very plausible. It is plausible whether or not Leftow is right that God creates possibilities out of his imagination. Human beings are not able to create possibilities, but we imagine a possible state of affairs in a different and superior way than when we merely understand a proposition. The function of the imagination in grasping possibilities is plausible for both objective and subjective possibilities, but I believe that it is the only way God can grasp possibilities from the first-person perspective of the bearer.

One thing I like about Aquinas's position that everything we say about God is by analogy is that it makes us humble about our speculations. When we speak of God's intellect and will, we imagine our own knowing and willing, and imagine God doing the same thing we do, only more so. When I say God imagines, I think of God doing what I do in imagining, only he does it with infinitely greater power. In each case, we start with our own finite powers and speculate about what the infinitely greater source of those powers would be like. We need to remind ourselves that we cannot be confident about the accuracy of those speculations. If we accept the doctrine of simplicity, that will force us to be even more humble in our speculations. According to that doctrine, there is no difference between God's intellect and God's imagination because there are no differences among any of God's attributes, faculties, or conscious states. Still, we do not refer to God's will when we ought to be referring to God's intellect, and it is in that spirit that I propose that we ought to be referring to God's imagination rather his intellect when we want to understand how God grasps the subjective features of the world.

Earlier in discussing the human imagination, I gave examples to illustrate how the imagination flows easily between the actual and the counteractual. Sometimes we know the difference and sometimes we do not. God has no trouble distinguishing them, and if the difference is vague, he has no trouble recognizing that. If there are causal relations between subjective and objective states of affairs, he can easily grasp those relations in his imagination. Connections between subjective and objective states of affairs are everywhere. Connections between one subjective state and another subjective state are everywhere. Connections between actual and counteractual subjective states are everywhere. The human imagination grasps counteractual beings and their subjective states, as well as one's own counteractual self, and that causes multiple changes in the actual world. All these connections can be expressed propositionally, but the imagination has the advantage of seeing the connections in the mind's eye, not simply knowing the fact that they occur.

If God grasps all possibilities in his imagination, it is plausible to say that God creates out of what he imagines. All possible objects exist in the divine imagination, and in the creation, some objects go from the darkness of the possible to the light of the actual. What, then, should we say about possible worlds? Theologians have always had the humility to admit that most of what we say about God is by analogy, either in Aquinas's sense, or in the weaker modern sense. I think that the same point applies to possible worlds discourse in metaphysics. The idea of possible worlds arose from an analogy with language, our most important tool for grasping both the actual and the possible. I agree with Leftow that for a theist, possible worlds cannot be nonreducible metaphysical entities like Plato's Forms. If they exist, they exist as clusters in the divine intellect, and they have only an analogous connection to human language. If the realm of the possible exists in the divine imagination, possible worlds in God's intellect are at best redundant. I am not proposing that we give up possible worlds semantics; it has been a very useful tool. But the theist has the advantage of adding to secular metaphysics the idea of a supreme mind. Even human minds do much more than know propositions, and a supreme mind can do all of that to a supreme degree.

My proposal that God imagines all possible creatures is neutral on whether Lewis is right that there is no difference between possible creatures and actual creatures. If we apply the Lewis approach to subjectivity, God creates all the creatures he imagines. God's generosity would extend to everything he has the capacity to create.[12] Like human women, God might regret that merely possible creatures are not actual. Not all possible creatures are compatible with God's goodness, but presumably many are. If all possible good creatures are actual, there would be no need for regret.

How do we know what is possible? We often face arguments that something is impossible because we discover contradictory elements in our system of beliefs. That has happened many times in the history of philosophical theology. Sometimes we think that something *should* be possible, but we cannot see how. We need to stimulate our philosophical imagination by considering analogies with something closer to human life that we think is possible. I used that method in Chapter 3 in arguing that God's grasp of actual subjective states is possible. My argument in this chapter is that God's grasp of counteractual subjective states is possible, but the lack of clarity on the nature of these states and how they relate to objective possibilities leaves us with much work to do in attempting to get a clear and coherent account of how they are grasped by God.

5.4. God's Counteractual Subjectivity

If God could have created a different universe, made different decisions, had different emotions (if he has emotions), and interacted differently with the human race, then it implies that

[12] It is interesting that when Leftow (2012, ch. 10) proposes an idea similar to this, he says that God is motivated to create in part by generosity. It could be argued that if God creates all possibilities compatible with his goodness, he is even more generous than if he created only one world. But Leftow argues that more is not necessarily better (2012, 290–298).

divine subjectivity could have been different. There are divine counteractual states.

The classical tradition of perfect-being theology includes extensive arguments pertaining to God's nature. God is eternal, perfectly good, omniscient, omnipotent, and simple. The classical tradition does not mention subjectivity in God, but divine freedom is also part of the tradition. Aquinas says that God can do what he does not (*ST* I q. 25 a.5), and he can do better than he does (*ST* I q. 25. a 6).[13] Most theists would agree, at least with the former statement. We ask what reason God would have to create, and what further reason he would have to create a particular world rather than another one that he could create but does not. We ask what reason God would have to permit evil, what reason God would have to become incarnate, what reason he would have to choose the particular form in which the Incarnation occurred, and many other questions. All these questions presuppose that God has a choice among alternatives, and because he has a choice, he must have counteractual subjective states. It also follows that he must have reasons for his choice, so there are reasons why the counteractual is not actual. God's reasons motivate him to act in one way rather than another, and we think that those reasons justify the action.

When we speak of divine reasons, that brings up the topic of the nature of reasons. Reasons are usually thought to be grasped by the intellect and shared with multiple intellects. They are understandable by any rational being who understands the circumstances, and justifiable from an outside viewpoint. That is to say, reasons are objective. Internalists, when referring to reasons, maintain

---

[13] The idea that God acted freely and graciously in the creation and in his providential governance of the world is an important teaching in traditional Christianity. Norman Kretzmann (1991a, n. 37) observes that Abelard was condemned at the Council of Sens for teaching that God could not do otherwise than he does. I recommend Kretzmann's interesting pair of papers (1991a and 1991b) in MacDonald (1991, 208–249). Kretzmann supports the Dionysian principle that goodness is necessarily diffusive, and so God necessarily created, although he argues that it was not necessary that God create the particular world he created.

that reasons must be connected to the subject's motivational states. Motivational states are subjective states. The issue between internalists and externalists about reasons is whether something can be a justifying reason for an agent if it is not connected to their motivating states such as desires and emotions. This controversy is interesting as applied to God because rarely do writers about divine reasons refer to the subjectivity of God. It is taken for granted that we can know what *kind* of state would be a reason for God even when we are not able to determine specifically what God's reasons are.

Externalists about reasons agree that reasons are usually connected with subjective motivational states. Internalists maintain that reasons are always connected with motivational states. It is uncontroversial that subjective states intersect with reasons, and so they intersect in God. Divine subjective states affect what God wills. If God acts freely, his choices could have been different; his reasons could have been different; his motives could have been different. The same point applies to us. This is one of the ways that our conception of the world changes when we see the prominent place of subjectivity in the universe.

Sometimes the focus on the divine nature in philosophical theology tempts us to conceive of God mostly in terms of what is necessitated by the nature of a supreme being. The idea that there is more than one possible way for a perfect being to act or think or feel is awkward, but it is obvious that the God of scripture is not a being who can be fully understood by a grasp of the divine nature, even if that nature could be fully and accurately described. It is not only free choice that requires divine counteractual subjective states. Being a person requires it, and if God is three persons, there are counteractual subjective states for each of the divine persons. I will offer my proposals on the subjectivity of the Trinity in the next chapter.

If God grasps the entire realm of possibility in his imagination, then God grasps all possible divine subjective states in his imagination. God can imagine what he could have done that he did not do, what he could have willed that he did not will, what he could have created, what he could still create if he wished. But notice that God could not imagine what he did not imagine since God imagines every possibility. I propose that the divine imagination encompasses all possible beings and all possible subjective and objective states for any being, including God himself.

God exists in the actual world, so God's imagination exists in the actual world. God's imagination contains within it all possibilities, so all possibilities exist in the divine mind within the actual world. I think that this can explain how we are able to see connections among the possible and the actual. Those connections are seen by God, and in our very imperfect way, we are able to see those connections ourselves through the participation of our imagination in the imagination of God.

In the history of philosophy, the imagination has usually been relegated to a secondary role in the economy of the mind. The intellect has almost always been interpreted as the superior faculty, with the imagination of little use in attaining truth, and even inferior to sensation. But the imagination has also been traditionally thought to be the locus of creativity and the faculty that connects the actual with the possible. I hope that there will be further work on the divine imagination, or at least a recognition that if we think that God has an intellect, we can say that God has an imagination, and if God has an imagination, he must use it for some purpose.

6

Divine Subjectivity and Intersubjectivity

6.1. The Trinity

Subjectivity is deep in reality. It clearly exists in abundance in the created world, and since the creator must fully grasp what he creates, he must fully grasp subjectivity in every form and in every detail in the world. God is omnisubjective. Only a being with subjectivity can grasp the subjectivity of others. So, God himself has subjectivity.

So far, I have discussed divine subjectivity as it is possessed by the one God who is the creator and providential governor of the world and the possessor of the divine attributes. My arguments for omnisubjectivity apply to all the monotheistic religions. In Judaism, Christianity, and Islam, God is one being, the unique possessor of the divine essence. The essence of any being is its objective nature. That nature can be shareable or not, depending upon the kind of being that it is. Creaturely essences are shareable. Divine essence is such that it can only be possessed by one being.[1] Included in that essence are attributes such as omniscience, omnipotence, omnipresence, and perfect goodness. These attributes are aspects of God's nature. God's omnisubjectivity is different because even

---

[1] If there are individual qualitative essences, as I argued in Zagzebski (1988), then only one being can instantiate your essence, and that is you. Your essence is not shareable. But even if there are such essences, they are all sets of properties that are individually shareable even if they are not shareable as a set. I think now that nothing qualitative can explain the uniqueness of persons.

Omnisubjectivity. Linda Trinkaus Zagzebski, Oxford University Press. © Oxford University Press 2023.
DOI: 10.1093/oso/9780197682098.003.0006

though it is entailed by omniscience and omnipresence and therefore must be essential to God in one sense of "essential," terms like "nature" and "essence" typically refer to something taken objectively. It is not possible that God is not omnisubjective, but divine subjectivity is not a component of the divine nature. It is a feature of the interiority of divine consciousness. Each of the divine attributes also includes interiority. God's omnipotence, omniscience, and perfect goodness are all features of divine consciousness. God's states of willing, knowing, and loving are subjective states, but we describe those attributes from the outside, often ignoring the fact that our third-person perspective leaves aside the first-person aspect of those attributes. There is something that it is like for God to think and to will and to love.

Another problem is that it is common in contemporary philosophy to interpret an essence as an abstract entity that is instantiated in individuals. Essences are sets of properties, and they exist in worlds in which the properties are not instantiated.[2] I have said that I do not think that subjectivity can be the instantiation of a property, and if so, omnisubjectivity cannot be an instantiation of a property. It is not an aspect of God's essence. Our subjectivity cannot be an aspect of our essence either; it is an aspect of our personhood. In this chapter I will offer my conjectures on the relation between omnisubjectivity and the doctrines of the Trinity and the Incarnation, and the infusion of the Holy Spirit.

I interpret a self as the bearer of subjectivity. A self is not a substance of which subjectivity is a property. A self is the inside of a person. The three Abrahamic religions all teach that God is personal. That is clear from their sacred scriptures and millennia of theology. The difference is that in Judaism and Islam, God is one person; Christianity teaches that God is three persons. Given that the doctrine of the Trinity was debated and defined long before the idea of

---

[2] See Plantinga (1979) for a landmark book on modality and essences in the framework of possible worlds metaphysics.

subjectivity entered philosophical and theological discussion, everything I say about divine subjectivity and the relation between a person and a self requires me to apply a distinctively modern concept to premodern writings. I have argued that omnisubjectivity is implied by traditional attributes and traditional practices of prayer, and I think that if the idea of subjectivity had existed at the time of the Church Fathers and the medieval theologians, they would have said explicitly that God is omnisubjective. If so, it is interesting to speculate about what they would have said about the subjectivity of the Trinity. Here I will offer my conjectures.

According to the doctrine of the Trinity, there are three divine persons, but one divine nature. This doctrine is beautifully expressed in the Athanasian Creed:

> This is what the Catholic faith teaches: we worship one God in the Trinity and the Trinity in unity.
>
> Neither confounding the Persons, nor dividing the substance.
>
> For there is one Person of the Father, another of the Son, another of the Holy Spirit.
>
> But the Father and the Son and the Holy Spirit have one divinity, equal glory, and coeternal majesty.
>
> What the Father is, the Son is, and the Holy Spirit is.
>
> The Father is uncreated, the Son is uncreated, and the Holy Spirit is uncreated.
>
> The Father is boundless, the Son is boundless, and the Holy Spirit is boundless.
>
> The Father is eternal, the Son is eternal, and the Holy Spirit is eternal.
>
> Nevertheless, there are not three eternal beings, but one eternal being.
>
> So, there are not three uncreated beings, nor three boundless beings, but one uncreated being and one boundless being.
>
> Likewise, the Father is omnipotent, the Son is omnipotent, the Holy Spirit is omnipotent.

Yet there are not three omnipotent beings, but one omnipotent being.

Thus, the Father is God, the Son is God, and the Holy Spirit is God.

However, there are not three gods, but one God.

The Father is Lord, the Son is Lord, and the Holy Spirit is Lord.

However, there are not three lords, but one Lord. (English translation from BeginningCatholic.com)

The Athanasian Creed emphasizes the unicity of God rather than the difference of persons, and it does not indicate the principle of distinction among the persons, so there is a multitude of interpretations on the difference between what God is as one being and who God is as three persons. Usually persons are interpreted as individuals, but the Creed says explicitly that there are not three individual beings. It is no wonder, then, that the Trinity is a mystery. Of course, a mystery is supposed to be unexplainable, but that has never stopped philosophers from doing their best to explain it. Interpretations have run the gamut from those that make God basically three and one being only in a trivial sense, to interpretations in which God is basically one and three persons only in a trivial sense. I will not engage with the many interpretations of the Trinity, but I want to say something about the concept of a person as a prelude to my conjectures on how the idea of a person connects omnisubjectivity with the Trinity.

Unlike the modern idea of a self, the idea of a person can be traced to the debates about the Trinity and the Incarnation in the early centuries of the Christian era.[3] The idea of *persona* was refined in order to have a way to define these doctrines, so the doctrines were not made to fit a concept that had already been well analyzed and elaborated. The fundamental insight that I see in the debates

---

[3] Rheinfelder (1928) is my source for this historical point on how the word *persona* entered Western discourse.

leading to the development of the idea of a person and in subsequent philosophy is that there is a difference between a *who* and a *what*. A person is a *who*. A nature or essence is a *what*. When we count beings, we count instantiations of essences. When we count persons, we count whatever it is that makes something a *who*. God is one *what* and three *whos*. Jesus Christ is one *who* and two *whats*. The difference between a *who* and a *what* was essential for both the doctrine of the Trinity and the doctrine of the Incarnation. It is interesting that we still distinguish a person from an individual human being in moral and legal discourse.[4]

Without the idea of subjectivity, the idea of a person had to be just as objective as a nature, and that led to intricate theoretical moves to explain the difference. The influential Boethian definition of a person as an individual substance of a rational nature explicitly states that a person is an individual of the genus substance (Boethius 1973, 85). That says nothing about what makes a person a *who*. It also leaves out something that became important in the way we think about persons after the idea of subjectivity was discovered: their uniqueness.

I said in Chapter 1 that my argument for omnisubjectivity does not depend upon my claim that the subjectivity of one person is necessarily different from the subjectivity of another. God would be omnisubjective even if it is possible that you share your subjective states with some other person. If so, that would mean that God knows the respects in which your subjectivity is shared. But I also believe that one of the most interesting ways in which subjectivity is important metaphysically and morally is that it can explain what makes each person unique.

---

[4] It is curious and somewhat ironic that the distinction between a person and a human being has been used by some philosophers such as Michael Tooley (1983) in defending abortion, and by others (Wise 2002) in arguing that certain animals are persons. Tooley's argument is that there are human beings that are not persons; Wise's argument is that there are persons who are not human beings.

The idea of the uniqueness of each person of the Trinity did not wait for a modern revolution. It was emphasized in the twelfth century by Richard of St. Victor (1959) in his critique of the Boethian definition of person. Richard defined a person as "an incommunicable existence of a rational nature" (*De Trinitate* IV, 23). By incommunicable, Richard meant that each person has something that cannot be shared with another, something that cannot be duplicated in another person. He does not, of course, mention subjectivity, but I suggest that since the incommunicable feature of a person cannot reside in their shareable nature, it must exist in their subjectivity.[5]

The incommunicable feature of persons makes them different from each other. Gradually over the last few hundred years, that difference has come to be treated as important and valuable. I have argued in other work (Zagzebski 2000, 2016b, 2021, ch. 4) that the rise of the recognition of the value of persons for their differences from each other accompanied the shift from a focus on persons defined by their nature to a focus on selves as possessors of unique consciousness. The shift from the objective to the subjective was important for the idea of human dignity. Originally, the ground of the dignity of persons was said to be their rational nature, the property identified by Boethius to distinguish persons from nonpersons. Rationality gives persons supreme, or at least very high value in the universe, but that cannot be what makes persons irreplaceable because rationality is a shareable property. It is communicable. I believe that there is another sense of dignity, that of irreplaceability, and in that sense, dignity is grounded in the unique subjectivity of each person.[6] What makes persons incommunicable in the sense Richard of St. Victor was attempting to identify is their subjectivity.

---

[5] See Crosby (1996, ch. 2), for a valuable treatment of the idea of incommunicability as it applies to persons both human and divine, and its relationship to subjectivity.

[6] I argue in Zagzebski 2016b that Kant attempts to combine the sense of dignity as supreme value with the sense of dignity as irreplaceability without noticing that they are two different kinds of value. In Zagzebski 2021, chapter 4, I offer a historical explanation for the two different grounds of the value of dignity.

I intend my brief excursion into the connection between a person and a self to call attention to the way the idea of a person as a *who* has developed over the last several centuries. That development affects the way we think of the personhood of God. Those who are originalists about the concept of *persona* in theology might think it right to ignore later philosophical work on persons, but that depends upon whether the later work is a distortion or a refinement. I think that discoveries about the nature of consciousness and its relation to value can be appropriately applied to God, at least by way of conjecture. High value and the value of irreplaceability are two different things. My position is that human beings have high value because of our rational nature. We have the value of irreplaceability because of our unique subjectivity. Likewise, I propose that God has the highest value because of the divine nature. Each person of the Trinity is irreplaceable because of their unique subjectivity. Even though the divine persons are identical in their essence, an essence that can only be possessed by one being, each person is a distinct self, and that means that their consciousness cannot be identical.

Aside from the Trinity, God is unique in the sense that the divine essence can only be instantiated in one being. Arguably, it is impossible that more than one being can instantiate the set of properties constituting the divine essence. For instance, no more than one being can be omnipotent because omnipotence implies power over every other being. But that is not uniqueness in the sense that applies to persons. An essence is the kind of thing that could in principle be shared by more than one being. Some essences are sets of properties that can only be instantiated in a single being, making that being one of a kind. The uniqueness of persons is different. A person is not one of a kind because there is no kind that it instantiates. If there is something different about each of us that makes us impossible to duplicate, that difference must be in our consciousness, and it cannot be something qualitative since a qualitative difference can in principle be duplicated.[7] What makes each person different from every other and hence irreplaceable cannot be anything in their objective nature. That difference must exist in their subjectivity.

I have said that a self is the inside of a person. If so, the definition of a person given by Boethius should be expanded to say that a person has an inside, and its inside is its subjectivity. As applied to the persons of the Trinity, that would mean that each person of the Trinity has a distinct self with its own distinct subjective states. Each has a unique point of view, a unique first-person perspective. Each has a different relation to himself than to the other persons of the Trinity. The Father, Son, and Holy Spirit each thinks of *myself* as distinct from *yourself* in the Trinity. The Father's sense of self is different from the Son's sense of self and the Holy Spirit's sense of self.

Aquinas's exposition of the Trinity is constrained by his metaphysical account of the divine essence.[8] He argues that the persons of the Trinity are distinguished only by their relations to each other, which are internal to the essence (*ST* I q. 28, a. 2–3; q. 29, a. 4). The Son proceeds from the Father and the Holy Spirit proceeds from the Father and the Son. The divine essence is communicated from the Father to the Son and then to the Holy Spirit without dividing the essence into three. There is one God because the procession from Father to Son is inside the Father; it is not the relation of cause to effect. Aquinas compares it to a concept or word proceeding from the intellect, where the word remains in the speaker, and that is why the Son is the Word (*ST* I q. 27, a.1, corpus). Similarly, the love between the Father and the Son proceeds within God:

---

[7] I think that the impossibility of the duplication of persons because of the possession of something nonqualitative can solve puzzles discussed in recent decades about the imagined duplication of consciousness and the identity of a person over time.

[8] For an impressively detailed account of Aquinas's theology of the Trinity, see Emery (2007).

The procession of the Word is by way of an intelligible operation. The operation of the will within ourselves involves also another intelligible operation, that of love, whereby the object loved is in the lover; as, by the conception of the word, the object spoken of or understood is in the intelligent agent. Hence, besides the procession of the Word in God, there exists in Him another procession called the procession of Love. (*ST* I q. 27, a. 3 corpus)

The Holy Spirit is the love that proceeds from the Father and the Son. The Son and the Holy Spirit are God because "All that is in God is God" (*ST* I q. 27, a. 3, reply obj.2).

Aquinas says that the members of the Trinity are distinguished only by their relations to each other, but if God is conscious, those relations imply differences in their consciousness. Differences of subjectivity are entailed by or supervene upon the relations Aquinas recognizes. Subjective differences are not intrinsic to the divine essence, and that make the members of the Trinity distinguishable in their consciousness. Each person is separately conscious of being known and loved by the others. The Father's consciousness of being loved by the Son and Holy Spirit differs from the Son's consciousness of being loved by the Father and the Holy Spirit.

Aquinas does not venture into a discussion of their individual consciousness and comes close to reducing the Son to something abstract: a thought or word, and similarly, he comes close to reducing the Holy Spirit to something abstract when he says that the proper name of the Holy Spirit is love (*ST* I q. 37). But a word is not a knower and love is not a lover. A word is not conscious, and love does not love. Aquinas is aware of this problem, and his answer is that there is no distinction between abstract and concrete in God: "For personal properties are the same as the persons because the abstract and the concrete are the same in God; since they are the subsisting persons themselves, as paternity is the Father Himself, and filiation is the son, and procession is the Holy Spirit" (*ST* I q. 40 a. 1 corpus). In reply, I suggest that consciousness adds something to the concrete that the abstract does not have. The argument that the abstract and the concrete are the same in God permits Aquinas to make the Trinitarian persons internal to the divine essence, but I think that leaves aside the distinguishability of the persons in ways other than their internal objective relations. I also think that their personal distinguishability explains much in scripture and subsequent theology.

Does God have one intellect or three? One will or three? Aquinas identifies both intellect and will with God's essence. So, there is numerically one intellect and numerically one will in God. Furthermore, there is one act of willing and one act of the creation, but the act is initiated by the Father, giving each person of the Trinity a different role:

> God is the cause of things by His intellect and will, just as the craftsman is the cause of things made by his craft. Now the craftsman works through the word conceived in his mind, and through the love of his will regarding some objects. Hence also God the Father made the creature through his Word, which is His Son; and through His Love, which is the Holy Spirit. And so the procession of the Persons are the type of the productions of creatures inasmuch as they include the essential attributes, knowledge and will. (*ST* I q. 45, a. 6 corpus)

Aquinas argues that God has numerically one intellect and numerically one will because God's power to think and will are identical with his essence. In addition, God's act of thinking and act of willing are identical with his essence. Given Aquinas's position on divine simplicity, that is what we would expect. All of God's attributes and acts are one and they are identical with his essence. But the act of creation is a cooperative act of the three persons. It is a single act arising from the idea of the created world in God's intellect that God wills to make actual by the Father acting through the Son and the Holy Spirit. However, this position does not force us to say that God has one self with one set of subjective states. Subjective states precede the formation of the idea of a world to create and the will to implement it.

So, is there numerically one intellect and one will in God? Aquinas must be right that essences include powers. The power of thought and the power of will exist in the divine essence, and both powers are perfect. The persons of the Trinity share one power of thought and will. There is also one act of knowing and one act of willing in the creation and in any divine acts pertaining to the created world. But some acts are cooperative, and Aquinas clearly thinks that the act of creation is a cooperative act with each person performing a different function. If that is the case, the point of view of the Father in the act of creation differs from the point of view of the Son and Holy Spirit, and I believe the difference is explained by their distinct selves with their unique subjectivity. But the three points of view are in perfect harmony. There is one act of the intellect and one act of the will because the union of subjective perspectives in God leads to one cooperative act.

Even human beings can experience something like the union of subjective perspectives. In close, loving relationships we might sometimes feel that we see together, form a belief together, and acquire feelings together. We can make joint decisions. Do we have one intellect and one will? No, but we have a union of intellects and wills in those circumstances in which our intellects and wills unite for a time. We can surmise that in God, the union of intellect and will in the Trinity is perfect, and that is compatible with three distinct subjectivities, corresponding to three distinct selves. A perfect union of subjectivity results in one act of will.

The difference in function within the Trinity is not limited to different roles in the creation, as we see in the Gospel of John before the betrayal and arrest of Jesus:

> If you love me, you will keep my commandments. And I will ask
> the Father, and he will give you another Advocate to be with you

forever. This is the Spirit of truth whom the world cannot receive, because it neither sees him nor knows him. You know him
because he abides with you, and he will be in you. (John 14:15–
17, NRSV).

Then later: "I came from the Father and have come into the world;
again, I am leaving the world and am going to the Father" (John
16:28, NRSV). Then Jesus prays: "Father, the hour has come; glorify your Son so that the Son may glorify you, since you have given
him authority over all people, to give eternal life to all whom you
have given him. And this is eternal life, that they may know you, the
only true God, and Jesus Christ whom you have sent." (John 17:1–3,
NRSV). Again, he reveals the work of the Spirit: "Nevertheless I tell
you the truth: it is to your advantage that I go away, for if I do not go
away, the Advocate will not come to you; but if I go, I will send him
to you" (John 16:7, NRSV).

Many centuries of reflection on these verses have led to the idea
that each member of the Trinity has a distinct role in interaction
with the human world. The Father initiates the creation; the Son is
the primary agent of the Redemption; and the Holy Spirit guides,
teaches, strengthens, and sanctifies human lives in the world
after the Ascension. These distinct roles are plausibly interpreted
as involving distinct subjective points of view, even distinct
personalities.[9]

In my article on omnisubjectivity (Zagzebski 2016a)
I hypothesized that each member of the Trinity has his own intellect and will, but they are in perfect harmony. In his response to
my paper, Bernhard Blankenhorn (2016, 453) objects, stating that
the traditional view of the Trinity affirms there is one single divine
operation in God because operation follows primarily from nature,

---

[9] Why three? Richard Swinburne (2018) argues that three persons are necessary for
the existence of unselfish love. Swinburne argues further that any fourth divine person
would be produced by an act which none of the three needed to produce. That person
would not exist necessarily, and so could not be divine.

not personhood. Blankenhorn's objection led me to rethink my
proposal about God's will and intellect. I agree that the powers of
the intellect and will obtain in one's nature, not one's personhood,
and so there is one power of the intellect and one power of the will
in God. But individual thoughts, motives, and aims are internal to a
person's consciousness and can be shared intersubjectively to produce a single thought or act of will. I propose that in God the execution of divine intellectual and executive powers involves both
individual consciousness and intersubjective consciousness. The
execution of the powers of nature is an act of a person or persons
working together. The subjectivity of each person of the Trinity
means that they execute a single shared power out of their own individual subjective states, and their intersubjective union explains
why they can agree in a single act of will leading to joint action.

It is possible for the consciousness of two or more persons to be
unified but not identical, and for the same reason it is possible for
two or more persons to separately direct their consciousness toward the consciousness of each other, and that involves separate
internal acts of will. But it is possible to have one act of will in any
joint action. There is one power of intellect and will, and one act of
thought and will directed toward the world in the creation, providential governance, redemption, and sanctification of the world.
But each member of the Trinity has his own unique consciousness that he directs toward himself and the other members of the
Trinity. So, I propose that acts of will in directing their internal consciousness differ from person to person, but it is their ability to direct their consciousness toward each other perfectly that produces
one cooperative act when they create and interact with the world.

I have argued that God is neither omniscient nor omnipresent
unless God is in some sense "in" the mind of each conscious being,
able to grasp what that being grasps in as perfect a way as is possible, compatible with a distinction of persons. On my hypothesis,
this point applies to the persons of the Trinity. If each person of the
Trinity is omnisubjective, each perfectly grasps the point of view

and sense of self of each other member of the Trinity, but does so in the way I have described, in which omnisubjective person A grasps the conscious states of person B as if from B's viewpoint, but never forgetting that A is himself. The Father perfectly grasps the Son's experience of suffering as if from the Son's point of view, but the Father is aware of being the Father grasping the Son's conscious state, and that is not identical to the Son's grasp of his own state. But the Son is also omnisubjective. So, the Son grasps all of the Father's conscious states from the Father's point of view, which means that the Son grasps the Father's grasp of the Son's conscious states. The same point applies, of course, to the Holy Spirit.[10] I propose that each member of the Trinity is perfectly omnisubjective of each other member of the Trinity.

The Trinity is a model of the most perfect understanding possible among persons, the most perfect understanding possible within a community of persons. The union of consciousness among the persons of the Trinity is perfect, and that is compatible with a difference in the point of view of each member of the Trinity and a different sense of self, the center of consciousness. What unifies them is their perfect grasp of each other, which explains why they are able to think, intend, and will together as one. Their perfect grasp makes possible perfect love among the three persons. Love is premised on understanding the other, and the fuller the understanding, the greater the possibility for love. The Trinity gives us a model of perfect love between perfect persons that is generated from perfect comprehension of each other. Similarly, God's love for each of us is generated from a preceding act of total, unmediated

[10] I have heard the worry that this position on omnisubjectivity within the Trinity leads to an infinite regress. The Father is aware of the Son's awareness of the Father's awareness of the Son's awareness, ad infinitum. I discuss a similar problem of a regress in the human mind's attempt to grasp all of itself in Zagzebski (2021, ch. 5). The problem arises under the assumption that there is a distinction between subject and object in every act of awareness. I doubt this applies to intersubjective awareness among the persons of the Trinity. In any case, even if there is an infinite regress of awareness, I do not see that as a problem. If God has an infinite mind, God can grasp an infinite regress.

comprehension of us. Omnisubjectivity is a condition for the perfect love God has for us, and its model is the perfect love within the Trinity.

The connection between creation and intersubjective imagination is very interesting. Many children have that in their fantasy play. When my twin sons were young, one of them could describe an imaginary situation in a few words, and the other one would immediately get it, and they would engage in acting out the fantasy narrative together. I think this can be a way to imagine how the joint creation of the world could arise out of the intersubjective imagination of the Trinitarian God. Each is a separate person with separate subjective states, but they are able to combine those states into a single imaginative narrative that they execute as one.

A stronger union of subjective states might even be possible. Max Scheler (2008, 12–13) has proposed that a perfect union of subjectivity can produce a single subjective state. He describes two parents grieving together at the funeral of their child. The grieving of one is not an empathetic sharing in the grieving of the other. They do not have two separate grieving states. Rather, they grieve together, and the grieving that was first separate becomes one state. *We* grieve, they would say. What they mean by "we" is a new subject of grieving, and Scheler proposes that they have a common subjective state created through intersubjective consciousness.[11] I do not know how we would be able to confirm that this happens, but I think that the possibility of this human experience can illuminate subjectivity within the Trinity. Each person of the Trinity has his own set of subjective states, but if parents can grieve together in one act of grieving in which the two of them together are the subject, the divine persons can think, grieve, love, and will together in one act in which the three of them are the collective subject. I do not know whether Scheler is right that two human subjectivities can

---

[11] I thank John Crosby for referring me to this example. He discusses it in Crosby (1996, 120–121).

merge in one subjective state, but it is much easier to think of that possibility in God.

The Creeds refer only to the difference of origin of the Father, Son, and Holy Spirit, without comment on whether there are other differences. I think it is important that a difference of origin does not preclude other differences. The differences of function that we see in Scripture suggest differences of consciousness, and we have seen some reason to think that intersubjective consciousness permits persons to think and feel as one. Even if it is only *almost* as one in human persons, that is close enough to show the importance of intersubjectivity as an aid to understanding how three selves can form a perfect union of thought and action.

Articulate mystics have given us images from their visions of the Trinity.[12] Almost all reports of Trinitarian experiences use metaphors or analogies. Some are taken from nature; some are human powers. For instance, William of St. Thierry describes his experience of the Trinity as memory, reason, and will (Hunt 2010, 9), which we see again in Bonaventure (Hunt 2010, 60). None of these three is a person. The same point applies to Hildegard of Bingen's vision of the Trinity as sound, word, and breath (Hunt 2010, 41). Julian of Norwich describes her inspiration upon looking closely at a hazelnut and seeing in it the work of the Trinity as maker, preserver, and lover of everything in the world (Hunt 2010, 108). We have already seen these functions of the divine persons, but the functions are not the persons. The objects of nature are not either. Geometrical analogies are even less helpful. They are constructed to help us imagine the possibility of three-in-one.

Teresa of Avila describes a vision in which each person of the Trinity was so real, she could describe and speak to each one while being aware of their one inseparable essence:

---

[12] See Anne Hunt's (2010) lovely book for a description and commentary on the Trinitarian insights of Christian mystics.

What was represented to me were three distinct Persons, for we can behold and speak to each one. Afterwards I realized that only the Son took human flesh, through which this truth of the Trinity was seen. These Persons love, communicate with, and know each other. Well, if each one is by Himself, how is it that we can say all three are one essence, and believe it? And this is a very great truth for which I would die a thousand deaths. In all three Persons there is no more than one will, one power, and one dominion, in such a way that one cannot do anything without the others. (*Spiritual Testimonies* 29, quoted in Hunt 2010, 139)

This is not as perspicuous as we would like, but at least it makes each Trinitarian person a real person who communicates with each other and with Teresa. Ordinary Christians address the Father, Son, or Holy Spirit individually in prayer or hymns, and my proposal that each person has a distinct subjectivity is a natural implication of those religious practices as well as of Teresa's vision.

Intersubjective experience is underexplored in philosophy, and I think that that is because of the trajectory philosophy has taken in the West. In Chapter 1 I gave a brief overview of the history of the objective/subjective split, which is usually described in terms of third-person versus first-person perspectives. The first-person perspective is the view from within one's own mind. The third-person perspective is the view from outside of minds. Some philosophers have suggested that these two perspectives lead to intractable conflicts (Nagel 1986), whereas others have attempted to include the subjective in a wide objective description of the world.[13] The idea that there is a second-person or intersubjective perspective has appeared from time to time, particularly in phenomenology, but it did not get much traction in subsequent philosophy.[14] I believe that

[13] Bernard Williams (1978) called that the absolute conception of reality.
[14] In Zagzebski (2021, ch. 6), I propose that intersubjectivity has the potential to solve our theoretical and practical problems arising from our inability to figure out how our individual minds fit into the universe as a whole.

the study and practice of intersubjectivity has the potential to help us in getting a coherent conception of the world as a whole. As a model for Christian lives, I think that it is helpful to see that there is a model of perfect intersubjectivity in the Trinity.

6.2. Divine Subjectivity and the Problem of Evil

The connection between divine subjectivity and the divine will has some interesting implications for God's reasons in creating and interacting with the world. In the last chapter I mentioned the connection between divine reasons and subjective motivational states. Here I would like to look at divine reasons for acting as they apply to the problem of evil. Statements of both the logical problem and the evidential problem virtually always include an alleged a priori premise to the effect that a perfectly good God would be motivated to produce good and to prevent evil. I have argued in another work (Zagzebski 2017) that as innocuous as this premise appears, it can be read in two opposing ways. We may all agree that:

(1) A good person aims to produce good and prevent evil.

But (1) has a hidden ambiguity. It can be interpreted either as:

(1a) A condition for being a good person is that she aims to produce good and prevent evil,

or as:

(1b) A condition for being a good or evil state of affairs is that a good person aims to produce the former and prevent the latter.

According to (1a), the good or evil of states of affairs comes first in the metaphysical or epistemological order. According to (1b), the good or evil of persons comes first, and the good or evil of states of affairs is derivative. Most writers on the problem of evil, both theists and atheists, interpret (1) as (1a). The logical or evidential problem of evil then takes off. But if God is the ultimate source and determinant of value, then the correct reading would be (1b). The ground of value is God in three persons. In *Divine Motivation Theory* (Zagzebski 2004), I argued that all value derives from something internal to God: God's motives. But we do not know God's motives a priori. We must look at narratives that reveal who God is and how God interacts with human creatures.

The difference between the two readings of (1) has parallels in other philosophical problems. To take one of the oldest, consider the famous Euthyphro dilemma. Euthyphro says: (2) What is pious is what is loved by the gods.

Socrates asks him which way we are to read that statement. Do we mean:

(2a) Something is pious because it is loved by the gods,

or

(2b) Something is loved by the gods because it is pious.

Likewise, we can say that a good person attempts to prevent evil because it is evil, or we can say instead that some state of affairs is evil because a good person aims to prevent it. Theists all agree that God is supremely good, full stop. I propose that it follows from that that states of affairs are good or bad because God is motivated to produce or prevent them. If we want to find out what is good or evil, look at what God does. If God is motivated to see something exist, it is good. If God permits something, it is tolerable (for reasons we may not understand). If God eliminates or prevents something, it is evil.[15]

If we now suppose that God has subjectivity, we can add something to my response to the problem of evil. Debates about that problem virtually always take for granted that reasons are objective. Divine reasons can be deduced from the objective nature of God. That is, a being with a certain nature would will certain things and not others. These reasons can be deduced by any rational being who considers God's nature. But if God has subjectivity, there are subjective reasons that cannot be deduced from God's objective nature as an omniscient, omnipotent, and perfectly good being. Some reasons are personal, arising from the distinctive perspective of a person, and those reasons are in the domain of the person's freedom. The divine nature is God from an outside viewpoint. There are indefinitely many choices compatible with the divine nature as we have been able to understand it. The choice that is actually made arises from the personal preferences and point of view of each unique self. We have the world we have because of personal choice, made intersubjectively within the Trinity. I am offering this as a hypothesis. It is one reason why the Trinity of persons is an important feature of the deity, and I think that it has the advantage of showing something deeply misguided in debates about the problem of evil. If we want to know what a person prefers, it is not enough to refer to their nature or essence. We see what they do. I think that we should do the same thing in attempting to understand God. We look at narratives of God as given in revelation and tradition.[16]

The motives of God can never be fully predicted from an examination of the divine nature, assuming we know what that is. If God is three persons, God has personality and unique subjective states

---

[15] If an evil was permanently prevented by God, we might not have any idea what it is. We might not even be able to conceive of it.

[16] This is a reason to endorse narrative approaches to the problem of evil such as that given by Eleonore Stump (2010).

out of which his acts occur. There are many things God could have done—an infinite number of things, but we want to know what God *did* do and why, and I think that means that we should be open to an investigation of the differences among the Father, Son, and Holy Spirit as those differences have been passed down to us and have been experienced by religious geniuses. I am not suggesting that we can get very far in understanding the subjective states of the divine persons, but I am proposing that realizing that those states are directly relevant to divine action can move debates about the problem of evil away from the focus on God's objective nature with its assumption that the goodness of God is derivative from the goodness or evil of states of affairs.

6.3. The Incarnation

Omnisubjectivity has interesting implications for the doctrine of the Incarnation. Other philosophers have observed that it would be odd if God had to become incarnate in order to become omniscient.[17] I agree. Likewise, it would be odd if God had to become incarnate in order to become omnisubjective. It follows from the nature of God that he is omniscient from all eternity, whether we interpret eternity as the timeless or the everlasting. Either way, omniscience cannot depend upon a decision to enter the created world in the manner in which the Son became incarnate as Redeemer. Similarly, God did not need to become incarnate in order to know what it is like to be human and to have human subjective states.[18] Does that mean that omnisubjectivity removes one of the reasons for the Incarnation?

---

[17] This point has been made by Sarot (1991).

[18] This means that I disagree with Eleonore Stump (2019), who writes: "through the assumed human nature of Christ, God can have empathy with human persons and can also mind-read them, since God can use the human mind of the assumed human nature to know human persons in the knowledge of persons way" (355).

In his paper on omnisubjectivity and the Incarnation, Adam Green (2017) argues that there is plenty for an omnisubjective God to learn through the Incarnation. Even though God already knew what it is like to be a human, the Incarnation gave God the knowledge of what it is like to be a human being who is God incarnate, and Jesus Christ also gave God the knowledge of what life is like for a perfect human. Further, Green suggests that Christ gains the direct experience of having a limited human perspective, and Christ learns what it is like *for me* to be tempted. My position is that God already knew all of that because he always grasped all possible subjective experiences in his imagination. He always knew what it would be like for him to have a limited perspective, to be tempted, to be a perfect human who is God incarnate. So, he does not learn anything new in the Incarnation. I think that the experience of becoming incarnate does not teach God anything; its importance is in teaching us something. Since we have no contact with God's infinite mind, we cannot know what God eternally knows. Would we even be able to *imagine* the Incarnation and the life of Christ if it had not happened?

Andrei Buckareff (2012) argues that the Incarnation would permit God to have knowledge *de se* of a human mind, which he did not have before, but since the Incarnation was not necessary, it was not necessary that God would have such knowledge, and that would mean that God is not essentially omniscient. He proposes that a Christian believer in essential divine omniscience should accept either panentheism or pantheism.

This is an interesting argument because I think Buckareff succeeds in showing that either God always had *de se* knowledge of what the Incarnation would be like, or Christians should accept panentheism. Buckareff does not mention omnisubjectivity, but if omnisubjectivity extends to the grasp of the counteractual, as I argued in the last chapter, there is a solution to his dilemma that does not force the Christian to accept pantheism or panentheism.

The Incarnation could not be motivated by the desire to gain new divine knowledge. But the actual subjectivity of Jesus Christ is a singular reality of monumental importance for Christians, and I would like to comment on its relation to the divine nature. Of course, traditional statements of the doctrine of the Incarnation do not mention the subjectivity of Christ, but the proclamation of the Council at Chalcedon gives us the constraints within which subsequent theologians have formulated their theories about the mind of Christ. Jesus Christ had two natures—one divine, one human—but was one person:

> Following, then, the holy Fathers, we all with one voice teach that it should be confessed that our Lord Jesus Christ is one and the same Son, the Same perfect in Godhead, the Same perfect in manhood, truly God and truly man, the Same [consisting] of a rational soul and a body; *homoousios* with the Father as to his Godhead, and the Same *homoousios* with us as to his manhood; in all things like unto us, sin only excepted; begotten of the Father before ages as to his Godhead, and in the last days, the Same, for us and for our salvation, of Mary the Virgin *Theotokos* as to his manhood;
>
> One and the same Christ, Son, Lord, Only begotten, made known in two natures [which exist] without confusion, without change, without division, without separation; the difference of the natures having been in no wise taken away by reason of the union, but rather the properties of each being preserved, and [both] concurring in one Person (*prosopon*) and one *hypostasis*— not parted or divided into two persons (*prosopa*), but one and the same Son, and Only-begotten, the divine Logos, the Lord Jesus Christ; even as the prophets from of old [have spoken] concerning him, as the Lord Jesus Christ has taught us, and as the Symbol of the Fathers has delivered to us.[19]

---

[19] Translation from Sarah Coakley (2002, 143).

An enormous amount of Christology since Chalcedon has focused on the issue of how it is possible for two natures to coexist in one individual person, but the attention has usually been on what a nature is and how two natures can combine, not on what a person is. It turns out that most of what is interesting about a person is included in nature, not personhood. The will goes with the nature, not the person, and so it follows that Jesus Christ had two wills: one divine, one human.[20] Similarly, the intellect goes with the nature, so orthodox teaching is that Jesus Christ had two intellects and two wills, but he was one person. On the traditional account, the personhood of Jesus is rather mysterious given that thinking and willing are not components of him as a person.

However, if subjectivity is a component of personhood, not nature, the personhood of Jesus Christ becomes very interesting. My hypothesis is that if Christ is one person, he has one self and one sequence of subjective states. There is one *I* since the *I* expresses the person. Christ could have had any subjective states possible for his divine nature, and any subjective states possible for his human nature, but divine subjective states were not simultaneously experienced with human subjective states. The fact that Christ had two intellects and two wills need not mean that they operated simultaneously. I propose that Jesus Christ had only one sequence of subjective states, the same as other persons.

There is more than one possibility for how this worked. One possibility is that Jesus never had any subjective states arising from his divine nature even though they were all possible since everything belonging to a nature is possible. He voluntarily gave up those states while on earth in order to fully experience being human. Those attracted to a kenotic Christology will find this in agreement with their theological perspective. Christ's awareness that he was divine might have been retained, but dimly, without

---

[20] The teaching that Jesus Christ had two natures but one will was the Monothelitism heresy condemned in 681 at the Sixth Council of Constantinople.

the subjective experience of his divinity. Another possibility is that Jesus Christ had predominantly human subjective experiences, but his divine will was still operative, and sometimes he willed to be aware as God. Or perhaps the Father initiated an act of the divine will that Jesus would have subjective states as the Son. There are many other possibilities. My proposal is just that as one person, Jesus Christ had one continuous sequence of subjective states as all persons do. He did not have a dual mind or a split mind or a split personality. He had a single *I* with the same continuity all normal persons have.

Thomas Weinandy (2019) discusses disputes about the *I* of Jesus Christ. He mentions the view that Jesus Christ had two *I*'s, one human, one divine, and the Thomist response that there was only one *I*, and that *I* was divine (2019, 404–405). Weinandy argues that Christ had one *I* and it was human. My response is that all these views misinterpret the connection between the *I* and a nature. The *I* goes with the person, not the nature, although the nature limits the possibilities of subjective experience for the person. I think it is a mistake to speak of a divine *I* or a human *I*, as if the *I* is a component of the nature. Rather, the person of Jesus Christ the Son is one continuous *I* from all eternity throughout the entire life of Jesus to his post-Incarnational existence. That *I* always had the divine nature, but he took on human nature for a time. There was no change in the *I* because there was no change in the person.

An important reason for the teaching that Jesus Christ had two wills is that it had to be possible that his human will conflicted with his divine will. Otherwise, the idea that Jesus was tempted does not make sense. That is a very plausible reason for the teaching that he had two wills, but it does not have the consequence that Jesus exercised his two wills at the same time. That would not be reasonable even if the two wills willed the same thing. Two acts of will from two different natures occurring simultaneously or in alternation suggests a mental abnormality. My proposal is that Christ's two willing *powers* existed simultaneously, but two acts of will did not.

That is plausible if I am right that Christ had one continuous sequence of subjective states as one person.

Imagine that you have such an abundant love of dogs that you want to take on the nature of a dog in addition to your human nature, and you find that you are able to do so. You have no wish to give up any part of your human nature. After all, you like being human. And you certainly do not want to become a different person. You want to remain yourself, the one person you have always been. You want only to take on the nature of a dog as an addition to your human nature, and to live for a time with dogs as one of them. And imagine that you do it. What would your life be like as a human-dog but with no interruption in your personhood? As the same person, you continue to be Maria or Steve. When you are born as a dog, you are, of course, given a dog name by whoever gives dogs their names. The dog-namer does not know who you really are, the person who preexisted birth as a dog, but that's okay because that is the way you want it.

You would need to block from your human awareness features of dog life that would be disgusting to you as a human in order to make your life as a dog a real dog life. You do not think both as a dog and as a human at the same time. Unfortunately, your life as a dog has some very unpleasant aspects. Sometimes other dogs do not like you and even want to kill you. A few dogs recognize something supernatural about you (above the nature of dogdom) and they flock to you and repeat your wise utterances. (I am assuming dogs can communicate with each other.) Eventually a pack of dogs kills you. You lose your dog nature but not your human nature and not your personhood.

In my fantasy I am leaving aside any motive to redeem dogs. I doubt that dogs need to be redeemed anyway. I am also not attempting any analogy with the Trinity. I am only attempting to find an analogy for the conjunction of two natures in one distinct person. As a dog-human you have two distinct sets of natural powers, and you are able to will as a human in addition to willing as a dog, but as a single person, you do not exercise your will as a dog and your will as a human at the same time. When you will as a dog, you have an awareness, perhaps only a faint awareness, that as a human you would will a certain way, but you are free to go against that will in your dog will. However, we can imagine that as a dog you never will anything that conflicts with your human will. You are a perfect dog.

If I am right that a person has a single sequence of coherent subjective states, then you have a single continuous sequence of subjective states before, during, and after your life as a human-dog. We can imagine that even before you assumed dog nature, you were able to grasp your pet dog's subjective consciousness perfectly. But your dog did not know that. If your pet and other dogs learn what you have done, you would have shown them the possibility of a transfiguring life in intersubjective experience between the race of humans and the race of dogs.

The debates about the Trinity and the Incarnation in the early centuries of the Christian era led to the important distinction between a person and an instance of a nature. If I am right that a person is necessarily unique, that must be grounded in the person's subjectivity. In contrast, a nature is objective. In the centuries since Descartes, the mystery of what a human being is has taken the form of the mind/body problem. Descartes thought that a human being is two substances, and that led to the problem of how they connect and interact as one. Even philosophers who gave up the idea of a soul or mind as a separate substance are left with the same problem. Consciousness seems to resist analysis as long as it is treated as an object in a world of objects, and the nature of conscious beings slips away from our investigations. The deeper problem, in my judgment, is not the connection between mind and body, but the connection between subjectivity and objectivity. Human persons combine subjective consciousness with an objective nature. Even though the Church Fathers did not have the idea of subjectivity, they made an important conceptual distinction. The separation of person from nature in the doctrines of the Trinity and the Incarnation applies throughout the universe.

6.4. The Holy Spirit and Divine–Human Intersubjectivity

If each person of the Trinity has a distinct subjectivity, each person of the Trinity is separately omnisubjective. But if we accept Scheler's example of the grieving parents, intersubjective consciousness can create a collective subjective state in which "we" are the subject. The Trinity as a whole is omnisubjective. Their intersubjective awareness of each other permits them to form a collective consciousness in which they can form a single idea and a single will to execute it. It also permits them to hear prayers together. That means that it is appropriate to address God as one, but it is also appropriate to address a particular person of the Trinity when we wish to pray to one of them with their individual personality and functions in mind. In an earlier chapter I mentioned my confusion when being asked by a fellow philosopher if I always pray to one person of the Trinity rather than another. I think now that it can be appropriate either way.

In Chapter 2 I observed that God's grasp of our subjective states raises the possibility of intersubjective union, a component of mutual love. In the Eucharist, it is possible that our consciousness is conjoined with the consciousness of Christ. Our relation to the Holy Spirit is different if the Holy Spirit unveils Christ but does not speak to us on his own (John 16:13, NAB). Still, when Jesus promises the coming of the Holy Spirit, he calls him the Paraclete (John 14:16, NAB), which is commonly translated as "consoler," and he calls him "the Spirit of Truth" (John 16:13, NAB). The Spirit inspires, guides, and protects the Church and the people of the Church. If the Holy Spirit is omnisubjective, how does that relate to these divine roles?

William Alston's (1988) paper on the indwelling of the Holy Spirit is a sensitive and penetrating study of models of how the Holy Spirit works within the individual in sanctification, with particular attention to whether the Spirit works inside or outside a person's soul in transforming their character. He begins with two models that appear in Christian literature and have some support from Scripture: the fiat model and the interpersonal model.

According to the fiat model, the Holy Spirit simply wills that a certain change be made in a human soul, and it is. God acts in the same way as in the creation, only his act is directed toward a particular human being. The change is made directly and apart from a person's consciousness. This model fits well with New Testament passages that refer to the moral changes in a person as a new creation or a new birth (e.g., 2 Cor. 5:17, John 3:3–8, NRSV).

In the interpersonal model, the relationship between the Holy Spirit and the human person is the same as between any two human persons who are able to influence each other, but of course, it takes a supernatural act to produce the kind of change the Holy Spirit makes:

> The distinctive thrust of the interpersonal model lies in its construal of the sanctifying work of the Holy Spirit on the analogy of the moral influence one human being can exert on another, by speech, by provision of a role model, and by emotional bonds. But all this leaves the parties involved external to each other in a fundamental way; they are separate and distinct persons, each with his or her own autonomy and integrity. (Alston 1988, 137)

Alston objects that both the fiat model and the interpersonal model lack the feature of internality that we see in the way believers are said to be permeated by the Spirit when they receive grace. The Holy Spirit is often compared to breath or air that fills a person inside them (1988, 138), and although Alston does not mention it, air is also suggested by the image of a cloud that overshadows Mary at the Annunciation. In the Catholic doctrine of sanctifying grace, we come to share in the being of God, participating in the divine nature (1988, 138). That suggests a much closer relation between us and the Holy Spirit than we see in the fiat model or the interpersonal model.

Alston calls his preferred model the sharing model. In this model "there is a literal merging or mutual interpenetration of the life of the individual and the divine life, a breakdown of the barriers that normally separate one life from another" (1988, 141). He observes that part of the sharing occurs below the level of consciousness (1988, 143), but he adds that the abundant testimony from people who feel filled with the Spirit in being overwhelmed by love, joy, or peace suggests that conscious states are a part of what is shared.[21] This is particularly apparent in the sharing of love:

> I suppose that the weakest internalization of divine love that could lay claim to being a sharing in that love, in a way that goes beyond the mere exemplification of a common feature, would be an immediate awareness of that love, the kind of awareness that one has of one's own feelings, attitudes, and tendencies. This would, indeed, be a sort of breakdown of the walls that separate different lives, a breakdown of barriers to experiential accessibility. (1988, 145)

That proposal clearly implies that there can be intersubjective union between God and human beings. God grasps our subjectivity and permits his subjectivity to penetrate our own. The breakdown of conscious barriers that Alston envisages is a part of the process of sanctification. If the process he describes is possible, omnisubjectivity explains why it is possible. If God is

---

[21] Alston (1988) adds an endnote (note 23) in which he comments that these feelings in people could be a reaction to the sharing rather than a part of what is shared if one accepts the position that the divine life does not include feelings.

omnisubjective, his decision to permit us to grasp, however weakly, states of God's consciousness is a decision to allow the grasp of another person's subjectivity to go both ways. I think it is also worth remarking that people do not experience this kind of merging as threatening to their identity. On the contrary, they find that the self is enlarged. That is important for those who fear that conscious union with any other being threatens to dissolve the self.

Although Alston was not a Roman Catholic, his sharing model fits well with the Catholic doctrine of sanctifying grace, as he recognizes. Aquinas refers to grace as a participation of the soul in the Divine Nature, "after the manner of a likeness, through a certain regeneration or re-creation" (*ST* I–II q. 110, a. 4 corpus).[22] The Catholic Catechism says:

> Grace is a *participation in the life of God*. It introduces us into the intimacy of Trinitarian life; by Baptism the Christian participates in the grace of Christ, the Head of his Body. As an "adopted son" he can henceforth call God "Father," in union with the only Son. He receives the life of the Spirit who breathes charity into him and who forms the Church. (Pt. 3 1197, italics in original)[23]

The Catechism does not refer to subjectivity; its conceptual categories are traditional. Alston also uses traditional concepts as far as he can. It seems to me, however, that once we introduce the idea of omnisubjectivity into theological discourse, we can get a much fuller and richer understanding of who God is and how God relates to us as human persons. We live our lives through our subjective states and the interaction of our subjective states with the

---

[22] In the sentence immediately following the above quotation, Alston refers to this passage of Aquinas by mistake as q. 100. It is q. 110.
[23] Catholic doctrine distinguishes between sanctifying grace and actual grace. Sanctifying grace is a habitual gift, a supernatural disposition that enables the soul to live with God. Actual graces are interventions on specific occasions (*Catechism* Pt. 3 2000).

states of others. Intersubjectivity is an intrinsic component of our relationship with other persons, and it should not surprise us that it is an intrinsic component of our relationship with God.[24] I believe that subjectivity is a more basic feature of reality than anything else, and I will explain why I believe that to conclude this essay.

[24] See also Stump (2019) for an account of the indwelling of the Holy Spirit in the mind of a person in a state of grace. Stump proposes that without losing her individual personhood or awareness that her mind is her own, the indwelling of the Spirit in a person allows shared mind-reading between them (2019, 360). Stump refers to recent work in neurobiology to illustrate the way interpersonal presence is possible.

7

Conclusion

The Primacy of Subjectivity

7.1. Being from the Inside and from the Outside

As a Christian theist, I believe that there has always been something in existence. That something is God. Everything other than God himself was created by God. God is personal, and persons have relations with other persons. There have always been personal relations in existence because the Trinity always existed. Persons have subjectivity, so subjectivity and intersubjectivity always existed. The created world exists because of divine subjectivity and intersubjectivity. God is a Trinity of free persons acting together, each of whom has unique subjective states as well as three-way intersubjective states. The concrete universe exists as the result of the intersubjective communion of the Trinity.

Much of this book has been about the contrast between the subjective and the objective. Does the contrast go all the way down to the deepest level of reality? Is there a real distinction between the subjective and the objective in God? Does the answer to that question have any implications for the connection between subjectivity and objectivity in the created world? In this concluding chapter I will suggest that the line of argument in this essay leads to a more radical position than what I have proposed so far.

One of my favorite lines in all of philosophy is Aristotle's proclamation that metaphysics is the study of being *qua* being (*Meta*

Omnisubjectivity. Linda Trinkaus Zagzebski, Oxford University Press. © Oxford University Press 2023.
DOI: 10.1093/oso/9780197682098.003.0007

bk. IV ch. 1). Being comes first. I like that because what we mean by being is neutral on what it is or who it is and how it is known. If being is or includes subjectivity, that would affect the way we investigate it. But after a good start, Aristotle goes on immediately to talk about substances, which are objective features of the universe:

> [T]here are many senses in which a thing is said to be, but all refer to one starting-point; some things are said to be because they are substances, others because they are affections of substances, others because they are a process towards substance, or destructions or privations or qualities of substance, or productive or generative of substance, or of things which are relative to substance, or negations of one of these things or of substance itself. (*Meta* IV, ch. 2, 1003b 6–10)

We speak of substances when we treat being objectively. We do that because we have been endowed with minds that need to classify in order to understand, and Aristotle does a magnificent job of classifying being into substances and their derivative features. But as Heidegger points out at the beginning of *Being and Time* (1962), being cannot be conceived as a substance or any kind of entity:

> Being, as that which is asked about, must be exhibited in a way of its own, essentially different from the way in which entities are discovered. Accordingly, what is to be found out by the asking—the meaning of Being—also demands that it be conceived in a way of its own, essentially contrasting with the concepts in which entities acquire their determinate signification. (1962, 26)

Heidegger repeats the Scholastic view that the universality of Being transcends any universality of genus. That makes it a Transcendental in medieval terminology (1962, 22). Being (*ens*) "transcends" the Categories of Aristotle, along with Unity (*unum*), Truth (*verum*), and Goodness (*bonum*).[1] In Aristotle, the Categories are objects of thought. Being is not an object of thought. It cannot be classified into a category, and it defies definition, as Heidegger stresses. We can treat it as an object, but when we do, we miss what is most important about it. My position is that if Being at the deepest level of reality is personal, it has an inside whether or not it has an outside. That means that the problem in understanding Being is not due only to Aristotle's particular system of classification. The method of classification itself distorts being because it is the treatment of Being from the outside.

According to Aquinas, the most fundamental thing we can say about God is that he is being itself (*ipsum esse*) rather than *a* being (*ST* I q. 4 a. 2, corpus, and passages quoted below). When we talk about beings, we talk about them from an objective viewpoint, as Aristotle does when he immediately moves from being to substances and their relations. Objectivity is an approach to being from the outside. Anything can be treated as an object, including our subjective states and the subjective states of God. Some things can only be treated as objects because they are unconscious. Presumably, there is no inside to a rock. But God only has an outside relative to us and any other created intelligences. It is because we are on the outside attempting to understand God that we say that God has an objective nature, one that can be grasped by human minds and communicated from one mind to another. In contrast, God's subjectivity is something God has and would have even if we did not exist. It is God from the inside. God from the inside is eternal. God from the outside is not since there was not always anything outside of God. It was *possible* from all eternity that there was something outside God, and God eternally knew that possibility

---

[1] These other Transcendentals are ostensibly coextensive with Being and differ from Being only conceptually. The early Scholastics debated whether Beauty is one of them. Many contemporary Thomists say yes, since Aquinas says that the beautiful extends to every being. All beings are and are beautiful through their form. See Cooper (2013) for an examination of Beauty as a Transcendental in Aquinas.

and what he would be like from the outside, but the actuality of God's objective nature depends upon divine choice in the creation; the actuality of God's subjectivity does not. God created objectivity when he created the world. Divine subjectivity was uncreated. That is one reason to conclude that subjectivity is primary. It is primary in God, and so it is primary in reality as a whole.

Although Aquinas did not conceptualize the distinction between subjectivity and objectivity, there are passages in his work that can illuminate this issue. One of them appears in his argument that God is undivided being. In the course of defending the view that God is one, Aquinas writes:

> Since one is an undivided being, if anything is supremely one it must be supremely being and supremely undivided. Now both of these belong to God. For He is supremely being, inasmuch as *His being is not determined by any nature to which it is adjoined*; since He is being itself, subsistent, absolutely undetermined. But He is supremely undivided inasmuch as He is divided neither actually nor potentially, by any mode of division; since He is altogether simple, as was shown above. Hence it is manifest that God is one in the supreme degree. (*ST* I q. 11, a. 4, corpus, italics added)

This passage gives us the interesting hint that Aquinas thinks that God's being is primary because it is undetermined by a nature. I interpret that to mean that it is not determined by any objective mode of classification. In creatures, being is differentiated into distinct natures—genus and differentia, individuated by created matter.[2] But the idea of a nature misses the mark when we get to the being who is not in a genus. There is no distinction between essence and being in God. Every other thing in existence has a contingent connection between its essence and its being. Its essence is

---

[2] Aquinas says that angels are not individuated by matter since they have no body, so they are differentiated by species. Every angel's species is distinct from every other.

independent of its being, so there is no necessity for the thing to exist. But God is a necessary being. God *is* pure being.

> Each thing is through its own being. Hence, that which is not its own being is not through itself a necessary being. But God is through Himself a necessary being. He is, therefore, His own being. (*SCG* I ch. 22.5)

A related reason God must be pure being is that God is pure Act:

> Being, furthermore, is the name of an act, for a thing is not said to be because it is in potency but because it is in act. . . . But we have shown that in God there is no potency, but that He is pure act. God's essence, therefore, is not something other than His being. (*SCG* I ch. 22.7)

I interpret these passages to mean that what God is God from the inside. It is God from the inside that is necessary.

For Aquinas, being is something that comes in degrees and individual beings participate in it. A being whose essence is not its being *is* by participation in being itself (*SCG* I ch. 22:9). A conclusion I draw from this Platonic idea is that human subjectivity is participation in divine subjectivity. In earlier chapters I proposed a way to think of omnisubjectivity in which God's consciousness flows through the universe, creating and conserving it as it flows. We could express that by saying that our consciousness participates in the divine consciousness. I think this respects the sensibilities of panentheists, but it is Thomistic in concept and terminology. When Aquinas explains his theory of analogous predication, he says that our intellects participate in the divine intellect, and our wills participate in the divine will. I have added the idea that our imaginations participate in the divine imagination. All our consciousness is caused by and participates in divine consciousness.

We are conscious in a sense that is analogous to the divine consciousness in Aquinas's sense of analogy.

God is being; therefore, being is metaphysically primary. We know that being has an inside; it has an outside only insofar as God is related to other beings. God does not think of himself from the outside. I assume with Aquinas that God is pure, undivided, and unlimited being. Divine being is maximal being. Before the universe was created, there was no being in existence except maximal being. There is no higher being. If so, since conscious being is higher than unconscious being, I conclude that God is maximal conscious being. Beings with lower consciousness participate in divine consciousness in lesser degrees. Beings without consciousness participate in divine being in an even lesser degree. If panpsychism is correct, even rocks and trees participate in divine consciousness in a minimal degree.

It would be mistaken to say that God is consciousness. As I mentioned in discussing the Upanishads, I do not think it makes sense to say that consciousness is conscious for the same reason that sight does not see, knowledge does not know, love does not love. A person knows and loves, so God possesses the consciousness of persons. God possesses maximal personal consciousness. As a Trinity, God possesses maximal personal subjective and intersubjective consciousness. All the powers of consciousness exist within God. Consciousness can be treated from the outside, but my arguments lead to the conclusion that God's being is intrinsically pure subjectivity and intersubjectivity.

We can reach this conclusion from another direction. Aquinas says that "Life is in the highest degree properly in God" (*ST* I q. 18, a. 3, corpus). Two paragraphs later he says "Wherefore that being whose act of understanding is its very nature, and which, in what it naturally possesses, is not determined by another, must have life in the most perfect degree. Such is God; and hence in Him principally is life." And in the next article he says: "In God to live is to understand" (*ST* q. 18, a. 4 corpus). Given Aquinas's psychological theory, understanding and willing are the two main operations of a living rational being. Operations of the imagination do not get his attention, but the arguments of this book lead to the conclusion that God's intellect and will are not superior to his imagination. Like his intellect and will, the power of God's imagination is infinite. In God to live is to imagine, understand, and will. If God has emotions, it is also to feel.

I conclude that objectivity does not exist of necessity. Subjectivity does. But I have interpreted the doctrine of the Trinity as implying that intersubjectivity also exists necessarily. The persons of the Trinity are subjectively outside each other, but not as one object is outside another. As humans, we are virtually forced to treat God as an object, even though we know that God is the supreme subject, or rather, three supreme subjects. At the deepest level of reality there is intersubjectivity. Intersubjectivity is more basic than anything objective. When we say that God is one, what we mean is that God is pure being that can be neither divided nor duplicated in another being. There can be no other being beyond pure being. Aquinas says that that is what it means to be one. God is a single infinite being with intersubjective consciousness. Each person of the Trinity has infinite subjectivity and intersubjectivity.

What would infinite subjectivity be like? When we speak of infinite knowledge, we mean knowledge with infinite breadth and depth. There is nothing to know beyond what God knows. There is no detail too trivial for God to know. Similarly, infinite subjectivity would be subjectivity infinite in breadth and depth. There is no possible subjectivity beyond what God grasps, and there is no item of subjectivity too small or too trivial for God to imagine. God's subjective reach extends to all possible sensations, emotions, thoughts, and choices. I have argued that this does not mean that God has your emotion of shame or fear, believes what you believe, or chooses what you choose, but all those states preexist in God's imagination in an infinite array of possibilities. Some of those possibilities are actual, and I proposed in Chapter 5 that God creates out of his maximal imaginative power. Of course, God does not directly create all actual subjective states since many of those states are created by free creatures. But none of them would exist unless God first imagined them and is continuously aware of them and continuously wills to keep them in existence.

What would it be like for God to have in his imagination an infinite range of sensations? We are familiar with the sensations arising from our five sensory faculties, but we can imagine indefinitely many sensory faculties, each with as many possible sensory states as that faculty can produce. If God has infinite subjectivity, God can imagine all those states and can choose the kinds of creatures he wants to create, each kind with a certain set of sensory faculties.

It is even more interesting to conjecture about the range of possible emotions. To me, one of the things that makes emotions interesting is that they combine a cognitive component and a component of feeling, as I mentioned earlier. It is mind-boggling to think of the infinite range of affective states directed toward all the ways in which the world can be perceived by any possible conscious being. I propose that God imagines every possible subjective state of every possible kind. All these states exist as possibilities in God's imagination prior to the creation.

If, as Aquinas says, God has infinite life, that suggests another interesting aspect of divine subjectivity. Writers have often observed that lives have a narrative structure. Aquinas probably did not think of that, but it raises the possibility that God's own life has a narrative structure. In fact, I believe that each person of the Trinity has a life with a narrative structure. The narrative would include a connected series of subjective and intersubjective states, and it would include providential plans for the creation and conservation of the world, the redemption of the human race and any other created races that need redemption, and a plan for the end of the world. None of this requires reference to anything other than the subjectivity of God—God from the inside. We talk about God from the outside, as I am doing now. We use concepts that we have developed from our common understanding of scripture and theology, all of which must be objective because we cannot get inside the mind of God. But if the inside of God is narratively structured, it is not enough to say that God is all-knowing, all-loving, all-powerful, and so on. God expresses those attributes the way persons do, in unique ways that form a story about desires and intentions, emotions and acts. I believe that God combines infinite consciousness with personal individuality. That is the wonder of the Trinity.

7.2. Intersubjectivity

Suppose I am right about the primacy of subjectivity in God. Would that have any implications for the relationship between subjectivity and objectivity in us? In Christianity and Judaism, a foundational principle connecting God and humanity is the idea of *imago dei:* we were made in the image of God. That idea appears with dramatic power in the first chapter of Genesis:

> Then God said, "Let us make humankind in our image, according to our likeness, and let them have dominion over the fish of the sea, and over the birds of the air, and over the cattle, and over all the wild animals of the earth."
> So God created humankind in his image,
> in the image of God he created them;
> male and female he created them. (Gen 1:26–27, NRSV)

For millennia, theologians and Biblical commentators have pored over these verses, attempting to interpret the ways in which we can be in God's image. Aquinas argued that human creatures represent their Trinitarian creator:

Every effect in some degree represents its cause, but diversely. For some effects represent only the causality of the cause, but not its form; as smoke represents fire. Such a representation is called a *trace*: for a trace shows that someone has passed by but not who it is. Other effects represent the cause as regards the similitude of its form, as fire generated represents fire generating; and a statue of Mercury represents Mercury; and this is called the representation of *image*. Now the processions of the divine Persons are referred to the acts of intellect and will, as was said above. For the Son proceeds as the word of the intellect; and the Holy Spirit proceeds as love of the will. Therefore in rational creatures, possessing intellect and will, there is found the representation of the Trinity by way of image, inasmuch as there is found in them the word conceived, and the love proceeding. (*ST* I q. 45, a. 7, corpus)

Aquinas thought that we have the divine image in our intellect and will, but neither faculty encompasses the whole person. St. Augustine offers a deeper image. He proposes that our faculties of memory, understanding, and will are the best analogue of the Trinity (*On the Trinity* bk. 10, ch. 11). The whole mind is in each faculty: "The memory is the whole mind as remembering; the understanding is the whole mind as cognizing; and the will is the whole mind as determining" (728). But Augustine says that the analogy fails because these three are not the only modes of the mind:

The ternary of memory, understanding, and will is an adequate analogue to the Trinity in respect to equal substantiality. But it fails when the separate consciousness of the Trinitarian distinctions is brought into consideration. The three faculties of memory, understanding, and will are not so objective to each other as to admit of three forms of consciousness, of the use of the personal pronouns, and of the personal actions that are ascribed to the Father, Son, and Holy Spirit. It also fails, in that these three are not all the modes of the mind. There are other faculties: e.g.,

the imagination. The whole essence of the mind is in this also.
(728, italics added)

Augustine implies that we have the divine image in our imagination. I have extended that point to say that we have the divine image
in our subjectivity and in our intersubjectivity with other human
persons and with God. The primacy of subjectivity in God makes
our subjectivity the primary way we have the divine image.

The lives we live can be told as stories, and if I am right about
what God is, we are all part of one big story and God is the script
writer. For millennia, stories were told from an outside viewpoint. In Chapter 1 I mentioned two important essays by Mikhail
Bakhtin (1981), who contrasts ancient narratives with the modern
novel and the change in consciousness that accompanied the
novel's invention. I attribute that change to the discovery of subjectivity. Narratives told from the inside viewpoint became the
norm, and we now believe that a story without the point of view
of the characters is hardly a story at all. In contrasting ancient and
modern consciousness, Bakhtin argues that for the Greeks, every
aspect of human existence could be seen and heard (1981, 134). The
Greeks did not distinguish what we call the internal from the external. What we call the internal was as visible and audible to others
as to oneself (1981, 136). In the novel, in contrast, the consciousness of the character is not only highly relevant, it is sometimes the
whole story. I believe that the change in consciousness reflected in
the switch from stories told from an external viewpoint to the focus
on the first-person standpoint in the modern novel should affect
the way we think of the divine narrative.

The story invented by God is created by the persons of the Trinity
acting together, so it is a joint story. The ultimate story of the world
is a cooperative story arising from intersubjective consciousness.
We can describe the creation of the world from the Big Bang on-
ward in the beguiling language of modern physics. We can pretend that we are witnessing the history of the universe when we

see videos of the expansion of the early universe and breathtaking photos from the James Webb telescope. It is enthralling to see the history of the created world as if we are witnessing it from the outside, but we are not seeing it as it was created out of the divine consciousness, and we do not know what it looks like from the divine point of view. From God's point of view it is a narrative, and it was created through intersubjectivity.

I think that awareness of the fact that intersubjectivity is the most basic feature of being should also affect the way we approach other people and other conscious animals. We are all tied together in God's consciousness, and the stories we create to give meaning to our individual lives are woven by God into a larger story that God creates. We have experience in creating joint stories in the ways we plan our lives with family and colleagues, and the ways we contribute to communities. We tell stories of family history, including the distant past, which I like to do because of my love of genealogy. We tell stories of the history of our art or science, our hobby, our university. We tell stories of our national origin. Some of these stories have been fractured, and the attempt to tell new stories is among the many challenges we currently face. Think how meaningless our lives would be if our self-created stories did not connect with the stories created by other people.

Where do we place intersubjectivity in our attempt to understand the world as a whole? Ever since the Scientific Revolution, we have made magnificent progress in giving an objective treatment of the physical world. The fact that this treatment has not been successful in explaining consciousness is a well-known problem. From what we know, it appears that consciousness is dependent upon brain structure, arising late in the evolutionary process. My point about the primacy of subjectivity is not about the order of evolution. My point is that we cannot explain subjectivity by starting with the world objectively described. This is not a point about the relationship between the physical and the nonphysical, but about the relationship between the objective, the subjective, and the intersubjective. We need a science of intersubjectivity. Such a science could not be empirical; that is an approach suited only to a study of the objective world. Phenomenology opened up a way of thinking about the relation between mind and world focused on subjectivity and intersubjectivity, but it never rose to the level of widespread cultural significance. I hope that we can regain the idea of intersubjectivity as a fulcrum for constructing a comprehensive view of the universe. If the God's-eye view of the world is the aim of inquiry, the aim of inquiry would be one based on intersubjectivity.

In a penetrating and very fair-minded book on the clash between subjective and objective viewpoints, Thomas Nagel (1986) argues that a host of philosophical problems have been intractable because nobody has figured out how to reconcile the subjective or first-person viewpoint with the objective or third-person approaches to the problem. That has left us with unresolved confusion about some of the deepest philosophical issues—mind and body, personal identity, free will, morality, the nature of time, and the meaning of life, among others. Nagel thinks of objectivity as coming in degrees representing distance from the self. For example, the subjective moral viewpoint is partiality centered on the self. We can assume greater and greater distance from the self in making moral decisions, representing greater and greater degrees of impartiality. The problem, Nagel argues, is that we know that something is gained by greater objectivity, but at the same time, something is lost. My response is that intersubjectivity is a point of view that has the advantage of linking to points of view outside the self, but at the same time, the first-person viewpoint is not lost in intersubjective exchange. I do not know how to apply intersubjectivity to the issues Nagel addresses, but I believe that if he is right that our history of philosophical debate on these issues reached an impasse because of the irresolvable clash between the first-person and third-person points of view, then it is likely that the systematic study and application of the second-person viewpoint is our best hope for getting a satisfactory approach to these problems that does not have the limitations of the first-person and third-person viewpoints.

In an earlier chapter I said that one way to pose the question of this book is this: How can God know us as subjects rather than as objects? Omnisubjectivity is the answer to that question, but now we see how misguided that question is. The primacy of intersubjectivity in God shows us that God knows us first as subjects, and only derivatively as objects, if indeed, he knows us as objects at all. Intersubjectivity is the glue of the universe. It is the reason that everything in existence is connected, and it is the reason that the ultimate goal of inquiry for us should be a map of intersubjectivity.

Omnisubjectivity is the zenith of intersubjectivity except in one respect, and that respect is important. Omnisubjectivity only goes one way. If I may offer a conjecture, or at least a hope, perhaps God's story of the world includes a final state in which it goes both ways in the Beatific Vision. I do not mean that we would become omnisubjective, but we would grasp as much of God's subjectivity as Aquinas says the blessed will grasp God's knowledge. A created intellect cannot see all that God can know and do since if it did, its perfection would equal God's (*ST* Sup. q. 92 a. 3 corpus). However, Aquinas makes an intriguing remark at the end of that paragraph:

> Thus the knowledge of the angels and of the souls of the saints can go on increasing until the day of judgment, even as other things pertaining to the accidental reward. But afterwards it will increase no more, because then will be the final state of things, and in that state it is possible that *all will know everything that God knows by the knowledge of vision.*" (*ST* Sup. q. 92 a. 3 corpus, italics added)

My interest is not in knowing everything God knows, but in sharing in divine subjectivity and the subjectivity of other persons, which in life is relentlessly blunted, sometimes tragically so. Many things need resolution at the end of time, not only the horrors movingly discussed in the theodicy literature. I accept the position that the resolution of all the suffering and evils in the world will come at the end of time, in the final chapter of the big story. Horrible evils get lots of attention, as they should, but I want to bring up the little bads that need to be healed or resolved, and which cannot be left dangling at the end of the world like loose ends at the conclusion of a flawed novel. Some little bads are forgotten but live on in some part of our psyches. There are many, many misunderstandings that are never corrected. A thoughtless remark hurts someone's feelings. The hurt is not permanent, but it is a hurt and it is not resolved. Some bads are important to a particular person, but have no effect on anybody else, such as forgetting a meeting with a person who was eagerly anticipating it.

Some bads affect a particular person deeply but do not involve extreme suffering. A woman loses an irreplaceable treasure, maybe her precious album of family photos. A young woman is very excited about the trip of a lifetime that she has been planning and saving for, and the day before she is to depart, the trip is suddenly canceled, and she loses the money she paid for it. A man is left at the altar by his intended bride after months of dreaming of their future. These bads are little in comparison to horrific evils like mass slaughter and slavery, but they are not little to the one who suffered them, at least for a time. Love is unrequited, the prize goes to someone else. As Dostoyevsky says in the mouth of Ivan, a final state of goodness is not good enough to make up for the cries of the little child who innocently and unresentfully prayed to dear, kind God to protect her from the beatings of her mother and father.[3] The beating of an innocent child or animal by people the child or animal loves cannot be removed by the later happiness of the child or the animal, much less by the later goodness of the world as a whole. I agree with that, and I think that the same point applies to every little hurt and disappointment. If there is a victim and a culprit,

---

[3] Dostoyevsky, *The Brothers Karamazov* (2022) bk. V, ch. IV, "Rebellion."

there must be a reconciliation between them that involves direct intersubjective exchanges between them. If there is nobody to blame, as in the loss of a cherished object, there must be a way that the suffering person can look at the event from a perspective that changes the place of the event in the person's own life narrative. Seeing the unhappy parts of our life story as components of a big story is not enough. Our life story itself can be changed and elevated. That requires intersubjectivity between each of us and God.

There are some little bads that are not known by anybody. Think of a man who loves a woman but never tells her until the moment before his tragic death. Only she does not hear him. Maybe there is a discovery that would have been a great benefit for the world, but it is overlooked. Nobody is hurt in these cases, and there is no actual evil that needs reparation, but it needs attention in the consciousness of the persons it affected or would have affected. Otherwise, the big story is not completed.

Is it true that at the end of the world everything will be revealed? I hope that it will happen, but I also think that it is not enough because the lost must be found, the broken hearts healed, the joys spread, and the meeting of minds and hearts completed. If everything that can make this happen is kept in God's consciousness like a treasure, then God can make it happen at the end of the world.

Bibliography

Alston, William P. 1988. "The Indwelling of the Holy Spirit." In *Philosophy and the Christian Faith*, edited by Thomas V. Morris, 121–150. Notre Dame, IN: University of Notre Dame Press.

Anselm of Canterbury. 1998. *The Major Works*. Edited by Brian Davies and G. R. Evans. Oxford: Oxford University Press.

Aquinas, Thomas. 1975. *Summa Contra Gentiles*. Translated by A. C. Pegis (bk. 1), J. F. Anderson (bk. 2), and V. J. Bourke (bks. 3 and 4). Notre Dame, IN: University of Notre Dame Press (cited as *SCG* in the text).

Aquinas, Thomas. 2012. *Summa Theologiae*. (Latin and English). Translated by Fr. Laurence Shapcote. Lander, WY: Aquinas Institute for the Study of Sacred Doctrine (cited as *ST* in the text).

Aquinas, Thomas. 2012. *Summa Theologica Supplement to the Third Part*. Translated by the English Dominican Friars. Second revised edition. Los Angeles: Viewforth Press.

Aristotle. 1984. "Poetics." In *The Complete Works of Aristotle*, edited by Jonathan Barnes, translated by Ingram Bywater. 2 vols. Princeton, NJ: Princeton University Press (cited as *Poetics* in the text).

Aristotle. 1984. "Metaphysics." In *The Complete Works of Aristotle*, edited by Jonathan Barnes, translated by W. D. Ross. 2 vols. Princeton, NJ: Princeton University Press (cited as *Metaphysics* in the text).

Augustine. 2012. *On the Trinity*. Translated by Arthur West Haddan. Veritatis Splendor Publications (cited as *On the Trinity* in the text).

Augustine. 1992. *Confessions*. Translated by F. J. Sheed. Indianapolis: Hackett Publishing (cited as *Confessions* in the text).

Baker, Lynne Rudder. 2013. *Naturalism and the First-Person Perspective*. New York: Oxford University Press.

Bakhtin, Mikhail. 1981. *The Dialogic Imagination: Four Essays*. Translated by Caryl Emerson and Michael Holquist. Austin: University of Texas Press.

Blankenhorn, Bernhard. 2016. "Response to Linda Zagzebski's 'Omnisubjectivity: Why It Is a Divine Attribute.'" *Nova et Vetera* 14, no. 2: 451–458. English edition.

Bobik, Joseph. 1965. *Aquinas on Being and Essence: A Translation and Interpretation*. Notre Dame, IN: University of Notre Dame Press.

Boethius. 1973. *The Theological Tractates and the Consolation of Philosophy*. Translated by H. F. Stewart, E. K. Rand, and S. J. Tester. Cambridge, MA: Harvard University Press (Loeb Classical Library series).

Bonomi, Andrea. 2008. "Fictional Contexts." In *Perspectives on Contexts*, edited by Paolo Bouquet, Luciano Serafini, and Richmond H. Thomason, 215–249. Stanford, CA: CSLI Publications.

Buckareff, Andrei A. 2012. "Omniscience, the Incarnation, and Knowledge *De Se*." *European Journal for Philosophy of Religion* 4, no. 4: 59–71.

Cappelen, Herman, and Josh Dever. 2013. *The Inessential Indexical*. Oxford: Oxford University Press.

Carrithers, Michael, Steven Collins, and Steven Lukes, eds. 1985. *The Category of the Person: Anthropology, Philosophy, History*. Cambridge: Cambridge University Press.

Carruthers, Peter. 1998. "Animal Subjectivity." *Psyche* 4, no. 3 (April) . journalpsyche.org.

Carter, W. R. 1982. "Omnipotence and Sin." *Analysis* 42, no. 2: 102–105.

Casey, Edward S. 2000. *Imagining: A Phenomenological Study*. Second edition. Bloomington: Indiana University Press.

Catechism of the Catholic Church. 1995. Second edition. New York: Doubleday.

Chalmers, D .J. 1995. "Facing up to the Problem of Consciousness." *Journal of Consciousness Studies* 2, no. 3: 200–219.

Chuang Tzu. 1964. *Basic Writings*. Translated by Burton Watson. New York: Columbia University Press.

Clayton, P. 2017. "How Radically Can God Be Reconceived before Ceasing to be God? The Four Faces of Panentheism." *Zygon 52*, no. 4: 1044–1059.

Coakley, Sarah. 2002. "What Does Chalcedon Solve and What Does It Not? Reflections on the Status and Meaning of the Chalcedon 'Definition.'" In *The Incarnation*, edited by Stephen T. Davis, Daniel Kendall, and Gerald O'Collins, 143–163. Oxford: Oxford University Press.

Cooper, John W. 2006. *Panentheism: The Other God of the Philosophers*. Grand Rapids, MI: Baker Academic.

Cooper, Travis. 2013. "Is Beauty a Distinct Transcendental According to St. Thomas Aquinas?" 2013 West Coast Meeting of the Society for Aristotelian-Thomistic Studies, unpublished.

Crosby, John.1996. *The Selfhood of the Human Person*. Washington, DC: Catholic University of America Press.

Cuneo, Terence. 2016. *Ritualized Faith: Essays on the Philosophy of Liturgy*. Oxford: Oxford University Press.

Daley, Brian E. 2002. "Nature and the 'Mode of Union': Late Patristic Models for the Personal Unity of Christ." In *The Incarnation*, edited by Stephen T. Davis, Daniel Kendall, and Gerald O'Collins, 164–196. Oxford: Oxford University Press.

Davis, Stephen T. 1979. "Divine Omniscience and Human Freedom." *Religious Studies* 15, no. 3 (September): 303–316.

Dennett, Daniel. 1991. *Consciousness Explained*. Boston: Little Brown.

De Vignemont, Frederique, and Jacob, Pierre. 2012. "What Is It Like to Feel Another's Pain?" *Philosophy of Science* 79, no. 2: 295–316.

De Vignemont, Frederique, and Singer, Tania. 2006. "The Empathic Brain: How, When and Why?" *Trends in Cognitive Sciences* 10, no. 10: 435–441.

Dostoyevsky, Fyodor. 2022. *The Brothers Karamazov*. Translated by Constance Garnett. Many editions independently published; in public domain.

Dougherty, Trent. 2014. *The Problem of Animal Pain: A Theodicy for All Creatures Great and Small*. London and New York: Palgrave Macmillan.

Easwaran, Eknath. 2020. *The Bhagavad Gita for Daily Living*. Vol. 1. Second edition. Tomales, CA: Nilgiri Press.

Easwaran, Eknath, trans. 2007. *The Upanishads*. Tomales, CA: Nilgeri Press.

Egginton, William. 2016. *The Man Who Invented Fiction: How Cervantes Ushered in the Modern World*. New York: Bloomsbury Press.

Emery, Gilles. 2007. *The Trinitarian Theology of St. Thomas Aquinas*. Translated by Francesca Aran Murphy. Oxford: Oxford University Press.

Flood, Anthony T. 2014. *The Root of Friendship: Self-Love and Self-Governance in Aquinas*. Washington, DC: The Catholic University of America Press.

Flood, Anthony T. 2018. *The Metaphysical Foundations of Love: Aquinas on Participation, Unity, and Union*. Washington, DC: The Catholic University of America Press.

Flood, Gavin. 2020. *Hindu Monotheism*. Cambridge: Cambridge University Press.

Frankfort, Henri, and Henrietta Frankfort. 1946. *Before Philosophy*. Baltimore, MD: Penguin Books.

Freddoso, Alfred J. 1984. *The Existence and Nature of God*. Notre Dame, IN: University of Notre Dame Press.

Frege, Gottlob. 1956. "The Thought: A Logical Inquiry." *Mind* 65/259: 289–311.

Fretheim, Terence E. 1989. "Suffering God and Sovereign God in Exodus: A Collision of Images." *Horizons in Biblical Theology* II: 38.

Friend, Stacie. 2016, "Fiction and Emotion." In *The Routledge Handbook of Philosophy of Imagination*, edited by Amy Kind, 217–229. New York: Routledge.

Gadamer, Hans-Georg. 1981. "On the Philosophic Element in the Sciences and the Scientific Character of Philosophy." In *Reason and the Age of Science*, translated by Frederick G. Lawrence, 1–20. Cambridge: MIT Press.

García-Carpintero, Manuel. 2017. "The Philosophical Significance of the *De Se* Attitudes." *Inquiry* 60: 3.

Gasser, Georg. 2019. "God's Omnipresence in the World: On Possible Meanings of 'en' in Panentheism." *International Journal for Philosophy of Religion* 85: 43–62.

Goldie, Peter. 1999. "How We Think of Others' Emotions." *Mind and Language* 14, no. 4: 394–423.

Green, Adam. 2017. "Omnisubjectivity and Incarnation." *Topoi* 35, no. 4: 693–701.

Griffioen, Amber. 2021. "Are You There, God? It's Me, the Theist: On the Viability and Virtue of Non-Doxastic Prayer." In *Reaching for God: New Theological Essays on Prayer*, edited by Oliver Crisp, James Arcadi, and Jordan Wessling, 38–58. Oxford: Oxford University Press.

Grim, Patrick. 1985. "Against Omniscience: The Case from Essential Indexicals." *Nous* 19: 151–180.

Hartshorne, Charles. 1934. *The Philosophy and Psychology of Sensation*. Chicago: University of Chicago Press.

Hartshorne, Charles. 1941. *Man's Vision of God and the Logic of Theism*. New York: Harper & Brothers.

Heidegger, Martin. 1962. *Being and Time*. Translated by John Macquarrie and Edward Robinson. New York: Harper and Row.

Houser, R. E and Noone, Timothy B., eds. 2013. *Commentary on the Sentences: Philosophy of God*. St. Bonaventure, NY: St. Bonaventure Press.

Hudson, Hud. 2009. "Omnipresence." In *The Oxford Handbook of Philosophical Theology*, edited by Thomas P. Flint and Michael C. Rea, 199–216. Oxford: Oxford University Press.

Hume, David. [1739] 2000. *A Treatise of Human Nature*. Edited by Mary J. Norton and David F. Norton. Oxford: Oxford University Press.

Hunt, Anne. 2010. *The Trinity: Insights from the Mystics*. Collegeville, MN: Liturgical Press.

Iacobini, M., I. Molnar-Szakacs, V. Gallese, G. Buccino, and J. C. Mazziotta. 2005. "Grasping the Intentions of Others with One's Own Mirror Neuron System." *PLOS Biology* 3, no. 3: e79.

Ibn Sina. 1892. *Books of Instructions and Remarks*. Edited by J. Forget. Leiden: Brill.

Ickes, William. 2003. *Everyday Mind Reading: Understanding What Other People Think and Feel*. Amherst, New York: Prometheus Books.

Jackson, Frank. 1986. "What Mary Didn't Know." *Journal of Philosophy* LXXXIII, no. 5: 291–295.

Jackson, Frank. 2003. "Mind and Illusion." In *Minds and Persons*, edited by Anthony O'Hear, 251–271. Royal Institute of Philosophy Supplements (Book 53).

Kind, Amy. 2013. "The Heterogeneity of the Imagination." *Erkenntnis* 78, no. 1: 141–159.

Kenny, Anthony. 1979. *The God of the Philosophers*. Oxford: Clarendon Press.

Kretzmann, Norman. 1966. "Omniscience and Immutability." *Journal of Philosophy* 6: 409–421.

Kretzmann, Norman. 1991a. "A General Problem of Creation: Why Would God Create Anything at All?" In *Being and Goodness: The Concept of the Good in Metaphysics and Philosophical Theology*, edited by Scott MacDonald, 208–228. Ithaca, NY: Cornell University Press.

Kretzmann, Norman. 1991b. "A Particular Problem of Creation: Why Would God Create This World?" In *Being and Goodness: The Concept of the Good in Metaphysics and Philosophical Theology*, edited by Scott MacDonald, 229–249. Ithaca, NY: Cornell University Press.

Kretzmann, Norman. 1997. *The Metaphysics of Theism: Aquinas's Natural Theology in Summa Contra Gentiles I.* New York: Oxford University Press.

Kripke, Saul. 1972. *Naming and Necessity.* Cambridge, MA: Harvard University Press.

Kripke, Saul. 2013. *Reference and Existence.* New York: Oxford University Press.

Kvanvig, Jonathan. 1986. *The Possibility of an All-Knowing God.* New York: St. Martin's Press.

Kvanvig, Jonathan. 1990. "Theism, Reliabilism, and the Cognitive Ideal." In *Philosophy and the Christian Faith*, edited by M. Beaty, 71–91. Notre Dame, IN: University of Notre Dame Press.

Leftow, Brian. 2012. *God and Necessity.* New York: Oxford University Press.

Lewis, David. 1979. "Attitudes *De Dicto* and *De Se*." *The Philosophical Review* 88, no. 4: 513–543.

Lewis, David. 1986. *On the Plurality of Worlds.* Oxford: Basil Blackwell.

Lewis, David. 1999. "Reduction of Mind." In *Papers in Metaphysics and Epistemology*, 291–324. Cambridge: Cambridge University Press.

MacDonald, Scott, ed. 1991. *Being and Goodness: The Concept of the Good in Metaphysics and Philosophical Theology.* Ithaca, NY: Cornell University Press.

Magidor, Ofra. 2015. "The Myth of the *De Se*." *Philosophical Perspectives, Epistemology* 29: 249–283.

McIntosh, Chad. 2015. "Review of Linda Zagzebski, *Omnisubjectivity: A Defense of a Divine Attribute*." *European Journal of Philosophy of Religion* 7, no. 4: 254–259.

Medeiros, Sylvia, Sylvia Lima de Souza Medeiros, Mizziara Marlen Matias de Paiva, Paulo Henrique Lopes, Wilfredo Blanco, Françoise Dantas de Lima, Jaime Bruno Cirne de Oliveira, Inácio Gomes Medeiros, Eduardo Bouth Sequerra, Sandro de Souza, Tatiana Silva Leite, and Sidarta Ribeiro. 2012. "Cyclic Alteration of Quiet and Active Sleep States in the Octopus." *iScience* 24, no. 4: 102223.

Meister, Chad. 2017. "Ancient and Contemporary Expressions of Panentheism." *Philosophy Compass* 12, no. 9: 1–12.

Metzinger, Thomas. 2003. *Being No One: The Self-Model of Subjectivity.* Cambridge, MA: MIT Press.

Michael, J. 2014. "Towards a Consensus about the Role of Empathy in Interpersonal Understanding." *Topoi* 33, no. 1: 157–172.

Morris, Thomas V. 1983. "Impeccability." *Analysis* 43: 106–112.

Motoarca, Ioan-Radu. 2014. "Fictional Surrogates." *Philosophia* 42, no. 4: 1033–1053.

Mullins, R. T. 2016a. "The Difficulty of Demarcating Panentheism." *Sophia* 5, 325–346.

Mullins, R. T. 2016b. *The End of the Timeless God*. New York: Oxford University Press.

Mullins, R. T. 2020a. *God and Emotion*. Cambridge: Cambridge University Press.

Mullins, R. T. 2020b. "Omnisubjectivity and the Problem of Creepy Divine Emotions." *Religious Studies* 58, no. 1: 1–18.

Mullins, R. T. 2022. "Impassibility, Omnisubjectivity, and Divine Eternality." In *The Divine Nature: Personal and A-Personal Conceptions of God*, edited by George Gasser and Simon Kittle. Routledge Press.

My Octopus Teacher. 2020. Documentary film. Pippa Ehrlich and James Reed, directors. Netflix original.

Nagasawa, Yujin. 2008. *God and Phenomenal Consciousness*. Cambridge: Cambridge University Press.

Nagasawa, Yujin. 2017. *Maximal God: A New Defence of Perfect Being Theism*. Oxford: Oxford University Press.

Nagel, Thomas. 1986. *The View from Nowhere*. New York: Oxford University Press.

Nagel, Thomas. 2010. *Secular Philosophy and the Religious Temperament*. New York: Oxford University Press.

Noone, Tim, and R. E. Houser. 2020. "Saint Bonaventure." In *The Stanford Encyclopedia of Philosophy*, edited by Edward N. Zalta. Winter 2020 edition.https://plato.stanford.edu/archives/win2020/entries/bonaventure/.

Nussbaum, Martha. 2001. *The Fragility of Goodness*. Cambridge: Cambridge University Press.

Otto, Rudolph. 1958. *The Idea of the Holy*. Translated by John Harvey. Oxford: Oxford University Press.

Perry, John. 1979. "The Problem of the Essential Indexical." *Nous* 13, no. 1: 3–21.

Perry, John. 2002. "The Self, Self-Knowledge, and Self-Notions." In *Identity, Personal Identity, and the Self*, 189–213. Indianapolis: Hackett.

Pike, Nelson. 1969. "Omnipotence and God's Ability to Sin." *American Philosophical Quarterly* 6, no. 3 (July): 208–216.

Pike, Nelson. 2002. *God and Timelessness*. Eugen, OR: Wipf & Stock. Reissue edition.

Plantinga, Alvin. 1979. *The Nature of Necessity*. Oxford: Clarendon Press.

Plato. 1961. *The Collected Dialogues of Plato*. Edited by Edith Hamilton and Huntington Cairns. New York: Pantheon Books. Bollingen Series LXXI.

Prior, A. N. 1962. "The Formalities of Omniscience." *Philosophy* 37 (April): 114–129.

Qur'an. *The Noble Qur'an*. https://legacy.quran.com.

Rameson, Lian T., and Matthew D. Lieberman. 2009. "Empathy: A Social Cognitive Neuroscience Approach." *Social and Personality Psychology Compass* 3, no. 1: 94–110.

Rheinfelder, Hans. 1928. "Das Wort 'Persona.' Geschichte seiner Bedeutungen mit besonderer Berücksichtigung des französischen und italienischen Mittelalters." *Beihefte zur Zeitschrift für romanische Philologie* 77. Halle: Niemeyer.

Richard of St. Victor. 1959. *La Trinité. (De Trinitate).* Edited by Gaston Salet. Paris: Edition du Serf (cited as *De Trinitate* in the text).

Rochat, Philippe. 2011. "What Is It Like to be a Newborn?" In *The Oxford Handbook of the Self*, edited by Shaun Gallagher, 57–79. Oxford: Oxford University Press.

Rogers, Katherin. 2020. *Perfect Being Theology*. Edinburgh: Edinburgh University Press.

Sarot, Marcel. 1991. "Omniscience and Experience." *International Journal for Philosophy of Religion* 30, no. 2: 89–102.

Scheler, Max. 2008. *The Nature of Sympathy*. Revised edition. London and New York: Routledge.

Scrutton, Anastasia Philippa. 2011. *Thinking through Feeling: God, Emotion, and Passibility*. New York: Bloomsbury.

Snow, N. E. 2000. "Empathy." *American Philosophical Quarterly* 37, no. 1: 65–78.

Stenmark, Mikael. 2019. "Panentheism and Its Neighbors." *International Journal for Philosophy of Religion* 85: 23–41.

Stueber, Karsten R. 2016. "Empathy and the Imagination." In *The Routledge Handbook of Philosophy of the Imagination*, edited by Amy Kind, 368–380. New York: Routledge.

Stump, Eleonore. 2010. *Wandering in Darkness: Narrative and the Problem of Suffering*. New York: Oxford University Press.

Stump, Eleonore, 2013. "Omnipresence, Indwelling, and the Second-Personal." *European Journal for Philosophy of Religion* 5, no. 4: 29–53.

Stump, Eleonore, and Norman Kretzmann. 1981. "Eternity." *Journal of Philosophy* 78 (August): 429–458.

Stump, Eleonore, and Norman Kretzmann. 1985. "Absolute Simplicity." *Faith and Philosophy* 2, no. 4: 353–382.

Stump, Eleonore. 2019. "Union and Indwelling." *Nova et Vetera* 17, no. 3 (Spring): 343–362.

Swinburne, Richard. 1977. *The Coherence of Theism*. Oxford: Clarendon Press.

Swinburne, Richard. 2018. "The Social Theory of the Trinity." *Religious Studies* 54, no. 3: 419–437.

Taylor, Charles. 1991. *The Ethics of Authenticity*. Cambridge, MA: Harvard University Press.

Tooley, Michael. 1983. *Abortion and Infanticide*. Oxford: Clarendon Press.

Torre, Stephan. 2006. "*De Se* Knowledge and the Possibility of an Omniscient Being." *Faith and Philosophy* 23, no. 2 (April): 191–200.

Velleman, David. 2020. "Self to Self." In *Self to Self: Selected Essays*. Second edition, 213–253. Cambridge: Cambridge University Press.

Voltolini, Alberto. 2013. "Probably the Charterhouse of Parma Does Not Exist, Possibly Not Even That Parma." *Humana Mente* 6, no. 25: 235–261.

von Balthasar, Hans Urs. 1986. "On the Concept of a Person." Translated by Peter Verhalen. *Communio: International Catholic Review* 13, no. 1: 18–26.

Walton, Kendal. 1990. *Mimesis as Make-Believe*. Cambridge, MA: Harvard University Press.

Weinandy, Thomas G. 2019. "The Hypostatic Union." *Nova et Vetera* 17, no. 3 (Spring): 401–424.

Weinandy, Thomas G. 2000. *Does God Suffer?* Notre Dame, IN: University of Notre Dame Press.

Wenders, Wim (writer, producer, and director). 1987. *Wings of Desire*. German film.

Wierenga, Edward. 1989. *The Nature of God: An Inquiry into Divine Attributes*. Ithaca, NY: Cornell University Press.

Wierzbicka, Anna. 1972. *Semantic Primitives*. Frankfurt: Athenäum.

Wierzbicka, Anna. 1996. *Semantics: Primes and Universals*. New York: Oxford University Press.

Williams, Bernard. 1978. *Descartes: The Project of Pure Inquiry*. London: Routledge.

Wilshire, Bruce. 2000. *The Primal Roots of American Philosophy: Pragmatism, Phenomenology, and Native American Thought*. University Park: Pennsylvania State University Press.

Wise, Steven. 2002. *Drawing the Line: Science and the Case for Animal Rights*. New York: Basic Books.

Wittgenstein, Ludwig. 1961. *Tractatus Logico-Philosophicus*. Translated by D. F. Pears and B. F. McGuinness. London: Routledge and Kegan Paul.

Wittgenstein, Ludwig. 2009. *Philosophical Investigations*. Oxford: Blackwell.

Wojtyla, Karol (Pope St. John Paul II). 2008. *Person and Community: Selected Essays*. Second edition. Translated by Theresa Sandok. New York: Peter Lang (Catholic Thought from Lublin series).

Wolterstorff, Nicholas. 1982. "God Everlasting." In *Contemporary Philosophy of Religion*, edited by Steven M. Cahn and David Shatz, 181–203. Oxford University Press.

Zagzebski, Linda. 1988. "Individual Essence and the Creation." In *Divine and Human Action*, edited by Thomas V. Morris, 119–144. Ithaca: Cornell University Press.

Zagzebski, Linda. 1991. *The Dilemma of Freedom and Foreknowledge*. New York: Oxford University Press.

Zagzebski, Linda. 2000. "The Uniqueness of Persons." *Journal of Religious Ethics* 29, no. 3 (Fall): 401–423.

Zagzebski, Linda. 2003. "Emotion and Moral Judgment." *Philosophy and Phenomenological Research* LXVI, no. 1 (January): 104–124.

Zagzebski, Linda. 2004. *Divine Motivation Theory*. Cambridge: Cambridge University Press.

Zagzebski, Linda. 2008. "Omnisubjectivity." In *Oxford Studies in Philosophy of Religion*, edited by Jonathan Kvanvig, 231–248. Oxford: Oxford University Press.

Zagzebski, Linda. 2013. *Omnisubjectivity: A Defense of a Divine Attribute*. Milwaukee: Marquette University Press.

Zagzebski, Linda. 2016a. "Omnisubjectivity: Why It Is a Divine Attribute." *Nova et Vetera* 14, no. 2: 435–450.

Zagzebski, Linda. 2016b. "The Dignity of Persons and the Value of Uniqueness." Presidential Address to the American Philosophical Association Central Division, in *Proceedings of the APA* 90 (November): 55–70.

Zagzebski, Linda. 2017. "Good Persons, Good Aims, and the Problem of Evil." In *Ethics and the Problem of Evil*, edited by James Sterba, 43–56. Bloomington: Indiana University Press.

Zagzebski, Linda. 2021. *The Two Greatest Ideas: How Our Grasp of the Universe and Our Minds Changed Everything*. Princeton, NJ: Princeton University Press.

Zagzebski, Linda. 2022. *God, Knowledge, and the Good: Collected Papers in the Philosophy of Religion*. New York: Oxford University Press.

Index

For the benefit of digital users, indexed terms that span two pages (e.g., 52–53) may, on occasion, appear on only one of those pages.

the Son, 51, 146–47, 151–54,
    155, 156–57, 160, 164, 167–
    68, 185

uniqueness, 18–19, 33–34, 51, 53–54,
    144n.1, 148–49, 150–51
Upanishads, 36, 40, 50, 54–55, 74–
    76, 181

Vedas/Vedic religion, 75–76
Vidal, Gore, 120–21

Webb, James, 186–87
Weinandy, Thomas, 168
Wenders, Wim, 8, 20–21
William of St. Thierry, 159
Williams, Bernard, 160n.13
Wings of Desire (1987), 8
Wittgenstein, Ludwig, 2–3, 12
Wojtyla, Karol, 19
Word, in God, 51, 151–52

"you" pronouns, 3–4